ONE PERFECT WORD

DEBBIE MACOMBER

ONE PERFECT WORD

One Word Can Make All the Difference

HOWARD BOOKS
A DIVISION OF SIMON & SCHUSTER, INC.

NEW YORK   NASHVILLE   LONDON   TORONTO   SYDNEY   NEW DELHI

Howard Books
A Division of Simon & Schuster, Inc.
1230 Avenue of the Americas
New York, NY 10020

First Howard Books hardcover edition January 2012

HOWARD and colophon are trademarks of Simon & Schuster, Inc.

For information about special discounts for bulk purchases,
please contact Simon & Schuster Special Sales at 1-866-506-1949
or business@simonandschuster.com

The Simon & Schuster Speakers Bureau can bring authors to your
live event. For more information or to book an event, contact the
Simon & Schuster Speakers Bureau at 1-866-248-3049 or visit our
website at www.simonspeakers.com.

Manufactured in the United States of America

10   9   8   7   6   5   4   3   2   1

Library of Congress Cataloging-in-Publication Data

Macomber, Debbie.
    One perfect word / Debbie Macomber.
        p.   cm.
    Includes bibliographical references (p.   ).
    1. Christian life.   2. Macomber, Debbie.   I. Title.
    BV4501.3.M238   2012
    248.4—dc23   2011028531

ISBN 978-1-4391-9059-3
ISBN 978-1-4391-9530-7 (ebook)

Contents

CONTENTS

To Susan Plunkett
My sister of the heart
My sister in Christ
My dear, dear friend

ONE PERFECT WORD

*If you remain in me and my words remain in you,
ask whatever you wish, and it will be done for you.*
—John 15:7

$\mathcal{O}_{ne}$

Upon My Word

Word (wûrd)
—**noun** A sound or a combination of sounds, or its representation in writing or printing, that symbolizes and communicates a meaning.[1]

I am often reminded of the power of words. In my office I have a number of author autographs lining the wall of my stairwell. Mark Twain. Harper Lee. Charles Dickens. Ernest Hemingway. Harriet Beecher Stowe. These writers are my mentors. As a young woman I read and cherished their stories. They remind me of my responsibility as a writer of fiction and most recently in my venture into the world of nonfiction. Indeed there is tremendous power in words.

Pearl S. Buck's novel *The Good Earth* actually changed foreign policy between the United States and China. When President Lincoln met Harriet Beecher Stowe, the author of *Uncle Tom's Cabin,* he is reported to have said, "So you're the little woman who caused the great war."

The definition I've given takes one of the most potent elements of communication—the word—and makes it sound almost innocuous. Yes, words have tremendous power. So much meaning can be packed into a word.

In the book *Simple Little Words: What You Say Can Change a Life*, Dr. Dennis Hensley tells the story of how one perfect word changed a life.

In my capacity as a professor of English at Taylor University Fort Wayne, I teach a survey course in world literature that students of all majors are assigned to take as part of their liberal-arts requirements.

A few years ago, I met Sean, a junior and wrestling-squad member who was majoring in elementary education. Sean had a shaved bullet head, legs like fire hydrants, a back that could put Atlas to shame, and biceps that looked like the drawing on boxes of Arm & Hammer Baking Soda. This guy was tough

Sean enjoyed sports, and he excelled at weightlifting and track-and-field events such as discus and hammer throwing. However, he wasn't overly keen on literature. I knew quickly I'd have my work cut out in making him an admirer of Keats, Shakespeare, Dante, and Melville.

I modified Sean's reading list for that semester to include high-seas adventures by Jack London, mysteries by Sir Arthur Conan Doyle, and military works by Rudyard Kipling. We met in my office once each week to discuss the books and short stories, and I constantly praised Sean's ability to recognize symbolism, foreshadowing, flashbacks, and other elements of literary expressions that I had lectured about in class.

As the semester advanced, so did Sean's grades. He had started as a C student, then rose to the B level. As I showed the class how the applications of literary analysis could help them better appreciate plays and movies, they all became more and more eager to get to class each day. Sean started sitting in the front row, taking copious notes, and I continued to compliment him on his diligence and studiousness.

Then, one day, as I was grading papers, I was delighted to be able to give a perfect A to Sean on one of his quizzes over a new short story I'd had the students read for that week. At the end of the quiz I wrote, "This is superb work, son. I congratulate you. You've been working hard, and this is the payoff. Well done!"

I passed the papers back, and I watched as Sean's face lit up in a grin when he saw the huge red A atop his quiz. However, when he turned the page over and read my personal note to him, his countenance changed entirely. He lowered his face, avoided eye contact with me the entire rest of the class, and left just as soon as the bell rang. I was thoroughly confused by such behavior until two days later.

During office hours, I glanced up to Sean's hulking frame taking up my entire doorway. "Can I come in for a moment, Dr. Hensley?" he asked me. I motioned him toward a chair, and he closed the door behind him. I could see that he had his quiz in his hand.

"Sir," he began, but then stopped. He lowered his head, and suddenly I realized that this giant of a man was actually weeping. I was stunned. I gave him a moment to collect himself. "Sir, you don't know my background."

I said nothing as Sean fished a handkerchief from his back pocket and wiped his eyes.

"My dad left my mom and me when I was only seven," Sean said in a low voice. "I somehow felt it was my fault that he left. I got it into my head that if I could just be a better son, my dad would come back and live with us again. We'd all be happy then."

He paused, then added, "So, I played every sport at my schools and all the summer sports I could sign up for. I thought that if I could just hit enough home runs or score enough touchdowns or shoot enough baskets, my dad would be proud of me and would come back."

"Did it work?" I asked gently.

Sean shook his head. "My dad only showed up at three of my games during ten years that I was involved in sports. It was no big deal to him. I tried my best to impress him, but I always felt that I'd failed. I haven't heard from my dad for the past two years, and I probably never will. I thought I had gotten past caring, until . . ."

I leaned forward a little. "Until what, Sean?"

"Until I got my quiz back from you day before yesterday," he said, looking directly at me. "You praised me . . . and you called me son. You might have meant it just as a passing catchphrase from an older man to a younger fellow, but it hit me like a freight train. I realized at that moment, that all my life I've wanted to have a man whom I looked up to, to tell me he was proud of me and to call me son. You have no idea what this note on this paper means to me. I plan to keep this for the rest of my life."

Sean wiped another sudden rush of tears from his eyes.

"I came here to tell you something, Dr. Hensley. I want you to know that I'm going to conduct my life from here on out—in everything I do—so that you will always be proud enough to call me son. I won't ever let you down. I promise you that. You've given me something that I've been yearning for my entire life, and I want to protect it."

He rose, and so did I. I shook his hand and gave him a manly hug, concluding with a slap on the shoulder. "You're a fine man, Sean," I assured him. "I have no doubt you'll make me proud of you in whatever you do in life."

A year later, Sean graduated with his degree in elementary education. He passed the licensing examination for Indiana and took a job in one of the worst elementary schools in inner-city Indianapolis. Most of the students there were from single-parent families, and all were desperately poor. Sean became a surrogate father to many of them. He would take his old van into the projects and ghettos and pick up dozens of children and take them to sporting events, Saturday movies, or vacation Bible school. He called the boys "son" and the girls "daughter," and they loved it.

In calling Sean "son," I not only changed his life, I gave him a focus on the ministry he wanted for his lifetime calling. He's now changing the lives of hundreds of other fatherless children.

Yes, indeed, one word of encouragement can change the world.*

---

* Michelle Cox and John Perrodin, *Simple Little Words* (Colorado Springs: David C. Cook, 2008), 25.

BREAKING IT DOWN

That's power. One perfect word. Yet in this information age words swirl around us every day. Tens of thousands of words—maybe a hundred thousand words on a crazy, busy day. We read newspapers, we check out blogs, we may follow Facebook and even Twitter. We respond to e-mail and we listen to real people talking . . . and talking . . . and talking. We drive with the radio on. We try to squeeze in time to read books and magazines. We may turn on the television at night. Words come at us incessantly.

But God says in Ecclesiastes 6:11, "The more the words, the less the meaning, and how does that profit anyone?"

Hmmm. Maybe we need to go on a word diet. My children loved Dr. Seuss's books, especially *Green Eggs and Ham.* Did you know that book grew out of a challenge? After Theodor Seuss Geisel, better known as Dr. Seuss, had written several books, his editor Bennett Cerf challenged him to write a story using no more than fifty different words. *Green Eggs and Ham* was the result. What a delightfully madcap story to be penned out of a strict word budget.[2]

So, what if, instead of tens of thousands of words every day, we meditated on just one book for a lifetime? That narrows it down. My NIV Bible weighs in at 727,969 words, according to the *New International Version Exhaustive Concordance.* Each year has a little more than 525,900 minutes in it. If we live to be eighty years old, that's about 42,000,000 minutes. If you subtract time for working, sleeping, and play, that still leaves a few million minutes. Meditating on one book is definitely doable in a lifetime, right?

But what if we focused on only one passage? I started memorizing Scripture years ago when I first moved to Port Orchard, Washington. Those were some troubling times for me. I didn't recognize it at the time, but I was going through a deep spiritual battle. In retrospect I look back on that battle and see it as a major milestone in my spiritual life because it was then I started memorizing the Bible. One verse at a time, I made God's Word a living, breathing part of who I am. I can't even imagine who I'd be today if I had not taken that step.

In 1999, I memorized the third chapter of Ephesians. In my prayer journal toward the end of that year I wrote,

> *Help me to know You more and more. Plant Your words in my heart so that all I need do is recall a verse and instantly feel its power, instantly feel the immeasurable sense of Your love engulf me. This year has been an incredible experience. Each day as I recite the passage I'm touched again by the sheer wonder and depth of emotion I feel in Paul's prayer.*

I closed my written prayer with a request: "May my own words touch lives for You." That one book, the Bible, has changed my life.

But forget whole passages for now. Let's break it down even further. What if I had one word—just one word—to meditate on for a whole day? How rich would that day be? Being a word person, I can't think of anything quite as fun as to luxuriate in one single word for the whole day, turning it around and looking at it from every angle.

And it doesn't have to be a complicated word. In his book *Orthodoxy*, G. K. Chesterton says, "Long words go rattling by us like long railway trains. We know they are carrying thousands who are too tired or too indolent to walk and think for themselves. It is good exercise to try for once in a way to express any opinion one holds in words of one syllable."[3]

God continues to tell us, "Be still . . ." In this barrage of wordiness, what does stillness look like? Maybe it means we take it one step farther and explore just one word for a whole year.

ONE PERFECT WORD

For almost twenty years I've been meeting with a group of women entrepreneurs for breakfast once a week. Many years back, my breakfast-club ladies and I decided to do just that: every January we've each selected a word to serve as a personal focus for the year. Over time the words I've chosen have had a powerful impact on my life.

But the title of this book is *One Perfect Word*. *Perfect*. Talk about pressure. If I was the one doing the word choice for each year I'd never be so bold as to call that choice *perfect*. The surprising thing is that when we decide we want to focus on one word for the year, God takes part in the choosing. That's why the word is perfect for us. We may not see it at the time, but as we look back we see that it all worked together—our word, our life, our journey.

When I find my word and begin to explore it, God takes me deep into that one word. Because I've kept journals nearly my entire life, I have been able to look back at them in the light of my word of the year and see how my life experiences dovetailed with my exploration of that year's word. Preparing to write this book has been an eye-opening journey.

In John 15:7, the Lord says, "If you remain in me and my

words remain in you, ask whatever you wish, and it will be done for you." That could be the story of my life. As I've tried to remain in Him and tuck His words deep in my soul, I've asked, I've imagined, and I've dreamed. The second part of that verse says, "Ask whatever you wish, and it will be done for you." I have to confess, God's blessed me far beyond that for which I have asked. Why should that be such a big surprise? That verse carries a promise. And God always keeps His promises.

When we choose one single word from His Word and spend a year with it, I've found that the Lord takes us by the hand and walks us through the year, teaching us about that word, about ourselves, and even more, about God Himself.

There are two things I hope to accomplish in the pages of this book. First, I want to encourage you to begin the practice of focusing on one perfect word each year. We'll talk about how to find the word, how to explore it, and how to recognize the life lessons that grow out of that exploration.

Second, I've chosen fourteen of my own words of the year to share with you. By telling stories that illustrate each particular word—some from my life and some from others' lives—and showing some of what I've learned about the word, I'm hoping you'll see God's fingerprints all over the exercise.

Sometimes my entries in my prayer journal over the years—my written prayers—express my one perfect word in the moment of discovery. In that case, you'll see the prayer set alongside the text.

Once in a while, I'll have a practical tip as to how to make a word come alive in a different medium. Some of us are more visual or tactile. I will share hints I've gleaned on making the word of the year tangible. You'll find those tips labeled "Wordplay" and set apart in a box.

CHOOSING THE WORD

In preparing for the start of a new year, I always go over my goals for the previous year, doing an intensive postmortem, so to speak. Which goals did I reach? Which did I exceed? Which do I need to rethink or restrategize? I usually read over my journals to get an overview of the year past. Often my word becomes clear during this time of introspection.

Sometimes, though, I don't get the word until a couple of weeks into the new year.

I'm not one for New Year's resolutions because they usually don't lend themselves to developing the strategy needed to carry them out. I am a goal-oriented person. I set goals and then go about devising ways to reach my yearly objectives.

Your word for the year is different from goals and resolutions. You don't necessarily choose a goal word like, say, *advancement*. The word is likely to be a complex concept that you will use throughout the year to explore a new aspect of your relationship with God and others. It needs to be something you will be happy to chew on for fifty-two weeks.

LISTENING FOR THE WORD

My friend, fellow writer, and plotting partner Rachel Hauck also chooses a word each year. Sometimes it takes a good bit of prayer for her to discover her word. This year, however, the word chose her. She told me,

> Throughout fall, the word and emotion of *joy* has been
> prevalent in my life. I had these waves of joy on Thanks-
> giving and the day before. The holiday saying on the

McDonald's cup was "Joy." My November book release was *Dining with Joy.* A worship CD came out about the same time entitled *Joy.* I went to visit friends in Nashville in December. Our hostess friend gave me an ornament with the word *Joy* stenciled on it. Earlier in the year, I gained a greater understanding of "the joy of the Lord is your strength" (Nehemiah 8:10). God's joy *is* my strength. He gives me His joy so I can be strong. A few weeks after that a friend gave me a mug that read, "The Joy of the Lord is my strength." She had no idea that had been a key verse for me in the spring. Second, Peter 1 talks about how we can actually partake of God's divine nature. So that's my focus this New Year, to partake of His divine nature in the realm of joy!

Needless to say, Rachel had her word. And she didn't even have to listen that hard.

By just picking one word, we start out with a simple "I can do that," and we end up with richness far beyond anything we've ever imagined. So come along with me and let's explore one perfect word together.

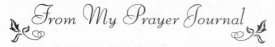

From My Prayer Journal

Dearest Lord, my prayer is that I might walk the walk with You in all things. May every area of my life be open and exposed to Your light. Every crevice illuminated by Your love. I want to hide nothing. To leave nothing concealed so that those who look at me might see a reflection of You and Your love. Amen.

May he give you the desire of your heart
and make all your plans succeed.
—Psalm 20:4

Two

DESIRE

De·sire [dih-*zah*-yuhr]
—verb To wish or long for; crave; want. To express a wish; to obtain; ask for; request.
—noun A longing or craving, as for something that brings satisfaction or enjoyment: a desire for fame. An expressed wish; request. Something desired.

The year I began keeping a journal as an adult was 1977. As the years have passed I spend time each December choosing a beautiful leather-bound journal, but more than thirty years ago, I was a young wife and mother struggling to make ends meet. That first journal I used during 1977 and 1978 was a spiral-bound notebook purchased off the school supplies rack.

The binding has let go from the top corner and the notebook is dog-eared, but the words are as familiar to me as the day I wrote them: "The deepest desire of my life is to somehow, some way be a writer. I should start with the pages of this journal to practice for the future. And the most important thing in my life is to serve the Lord Jesus Christ, my Savior." I had not yet started to formally choose a word in 1977, but as I read over that journal, I could see that God had chosen a word for me to explore that year: *desire*. The word was woven throughout the entire year. In the first short passage from January 1, I used the word *desire* four different times.

THE POWER OF NAMING YOUR DESIRE

"The deepest desire of my life is to somehow, some way be a writer." That sounds like a straightforward dream. Many people want to write a book. For me, however, putting words to that desire took real courage. You'd be hard-pressed to find a more unlikely writer. If you've read my other nonfiction books or heard me speak, you've heard the story of my journey to publication, but I'm retelling it because it illustrates what God can do with what most would call a totally unrealistic desire. While struggling to sell my first book I came to realize that God most often uses our weaknesses instead of our strengths.

As a child of the fifties growing up in Yakima, Washington, I found that words were both my passion and my torment. My mom said that from the time I was four years old, I went to sleep each night with a book in my hands. I visited the local library every chance I got. Beverly Bunn, the children's librarian, would read to us for story hour. She later married and went on to write novels, too. You may have read her work. Her married name is Beverly Cleary.

Despite my love for stories and for reading, I've always struggled in school. I was the only girl in my first-grade class placed with the "robins," the very lowest-level reading group.

Year after year I stayed in the low group. I still remember sitting with my mother at a parent-teacher conference when my third-grade teacher said, "Debbie's a nice little girl, but she'll never do well in school." Whether it was a self-fulfilling prophecy, I don't know, but she was right; I never achieved high grades no matter how hard I tried. I remained an average student, so average in fact that I ranked fortieth in a class of eighty girls.

In the 1950s, teachers didn't recognize dyslexia. Only much later, when two of my own children were diagnosed with the learning disorder, did I recognize that their reading difficulties mirrored my own.

The biggest complaint teachers voiced about me was that I daydreamed too much. It was true. As early as I can remember, I created stories, often when I was supposed to be paying attention in class. Storytelling actually became my niche when I was twelve or thirteen and had babysitting jobs. I used to make up stories about the kids I watched, giving them silly names like Snickelfritz and Stinkyfoot. They loved it. I became so much in demand that parents would pay me a dollar an hour when the going rate was just a quarter.

Though reading was difficult, I persisted. I was in fifth grade before I understood the concept of sounding out words. I was ten when I started thinking about what it would be like to be a writer. I wrote my first book the following year.

I still remember the characters—the story was about triplets named Faith, Hope, and Charity—but I never showed it to anyone. I was too afraid they would laugh, and I couldn't bear to have anyone crush my fragile dream of one day writing novels.

PUTTING FEET TO YOUR DREAMS

About eighteen months after I confessed my lifelong desire in my journal back in 1977, my cousin David died of leukemia. We'd been especially close and his death rocked my world. I realized life holds no guarantees. It was time to put my desire front and center. It was time to pursue my dream. Since we didn't have the money to buy a typewriter, we rented one. Every morning when the two older kids left for school, I'd move the typewriter to the kitchen table and write until they came home. I didn't have a lot of life experience at that point, but I knew I could write something with a happy ending. And, after four kids, I needed a happy ending.

I wrote for two and a half years with only rejections to show for all my effort. Then one Sunday my husband, Wayne, came to me. Before he said a word one look at his face told me it was bad news. He hesitated for a long minute and said, "Honey, I'm sorry, but I have to ask you to find a job."

It was early 1980. I can still see it as if it were yesterday. Wayne stood in the kitchen doorway, clutching a handful of bills. My stomach clenched and I swallowed an automatic protest as I saw the look of regret in his eyes. I knew it was hard for Wayne to ask me to find a job, but I also knew we were going deeper into debt each month while I struggled to sell my first novel. I thought about how hard I had worked since David's death. I hadn't politely tried to tap against the door of opportunity—I had thrown the full force of my determination into it. Despite the rejections and the times I had wondered whether I had the talent or grit to get there, I'd kept going. Over and over I had rammed this dream against an impenetrable wall of doubts.

But everything came crashing to a halt as Wayne set down the unpaid bills in front of me. Together we reviewed our finances and I realized there wasn't any alternative. I had to get a job, a real job, one that would contribute to our family income.

So, with the newspaper in hand, I circled three positions to apply for the next morning. Because I'd married as a teenager, I didn't have any marketable job skills. Even if I was fortunate enough to get hired right away, I'd be lucky to receive anything above minimum wage.

As I looked up from the newspaper, my gaze fell on the typewriter and I knew this would be the end of my hopes and dreams of ever selling a novel. All four of the children were involved in sports, music, Scouts, and church. There simply weren't enough hours in the day for me to keep up with the kids' wacky schedules, work forty hours a week, maintain the house, and still write.

Doubts battered me from all sides as I circled those three jobs in the newspaper. There was a swing shift opening at the A&P. A dentist was looking for a receptionist. And the local cleaners had placed an ad in the paper. I wasn't sure what my job would be there. Don't misunderstand me. There was nothing wrong with any of these jobs; they were the only ones I felt qualified to apply for. Yet, deep down I knew that I was born to write. Now, however, it looked as if that dream would have to be put on hold.

I remember going to bed that night, trying not to let Wayne know how depressed and miserable I was. In the darkness, with Wayne sleeping softly at my side, I recalled the joy and enthusiasm I'd had as I began this venture. Despite everything, I felt so sure God was leading me to write novels. I was willing to tackle every obstacle, every doubt. With my Bible and a copy of Norman Vincent Peale's *The Power of Positive Thinking* at my side, I was certain that sooner or later a New York publisher would recognize my talent and offer me a contract.

Go for It!

I had refused to give up, and yet, here I was, two and a half years into the journey, and I hadn't sold a single word. Instead of contributing to our family income, I was draining our already meager finances. I just never believed it would end like this.

As hard as I tried, I couldn't sleep. In the darkness, I prayed and offered this desire back to God. He was the one who'd given it to me in the first place and I'd gone as far with it as I humanly could. The rest was up to Him. Perhaps someday I'd be able to write again.

About two or three in the morning, Wayne rolled over and whispered, "Are you awake?"

"I haven't been to sleep yet," I confessed.

He waited a moment and then asked, "What's wrong?"

My heart was so heavy that I blurted out the truth. "You know, I really think I could have made it as a writer."

Wayne didn't say anything for a long time. Then he sat up and turned on the light. An eternity passed before he said, "All right, honey, go for it. We'll make whatever sacrifices we need to make."

How fortunate I am to have a husband who was willing to believe in me.

I wish I could tell you it was only a matter of a few weeks before New York recognized my talent and offered me that first contract. It was another two and a half years of budgeting dif-

ficulties and financial struggles before I sold. Almost five years
passed between the day we rented the typewriter and that long-
awaited phone call from New York. Five long years.

In those early years, I wrote four complete novels, each one
receiving a stack of rejections. I used to tell people I got rejected
so fast the manuscripts practically hit me in the back of the head
on the way home from the post office. About halfway through
that long dry stretch, while Wayne so lovingly supported me
despite the drain I was creating on our family's finances, I realized that I needed to start contributing to our family's income.
I started selling magazine articles. In 1982, I sold a small piece
to *Woman's World* and was paid $300—more than I'd ever re-
ceived. It was enough to pay my way to attend my first writer's
conference, put on by the Pacific Northwest Writers.

Two editors from a major romance publisher were scheduled
to attend this conference. They offered to review ten manuscripts. Writers were invited to submit a proposal to be critiqued
by these editors. I still remember the day I received notification
that my manuscript had been one of those chosen by the editors.
A strange feeling came over me unlike anything I'd ever experienced before or since. I knew that I knew that I knew. "I'm going
to make it," I told my husband. "I'm going to sell this book."

The first day of the conference arrived and I found myself
crammed into a workshop with three hundred other writers, all
as eager and excited about selling their stories as I was. The two
editors introduced themselves and then claimed that of the ten
manuscripts they would be reviewing, only one of them showed
promise.

I knew it was mine. I was positive. It was a foregone con-
clusion. In my heart, I knew. After all, I'd invested nearly five
years at this point. My story was good. Actually, it was great. I'd

rewritten it until it shone so brightly there was a danger it might blind the editor with the dazzling light of my genius.

Did I ever have a wake-up call coming.

PURSUING THE DREAM
DESPITE THE NAYSAYERS

As you may have guessed, the manuscript the editor liked wasn't mine. When she started to discuss my story, she had the entire room laughing at what she called the sheer implausibility of my plot.

After the workshop was over, I swallowed my pride and humbly made my way over to the editor. I explained who I was and which story was mine. I asked her if she would be willing to review my manuscript again if I rewrote the proposal. As long as I live, I'll never forget the look of pity that came over her face. She leaned forward, pressed her hand on my arm, and said, "Honey, throw it away."

Throw it away.

That proposal was as perfect as I could make it. It was the very best I was capable of writing. After investing nearly five years of my life in writing, in pursuing my dream, someone thought I should throw it away, like worn-out shoes or a rusty bicycle?

That night I returned home, defeated. These were hard times for the Macomber family. My husband, an electrician, had been out of work for several weeks. He'd gone up to Alaska hoping to get out on the pipeline. He was living in Fairbanks, eating one meal a day, while the children and I remained in Seattle, living off his unemployment check of $150 a week.

Try as I might, I couldn't sleep. About three in the morning,

I sat alone in our living room and watched the shadows on the wall. They seemed to taunt me. "So you think you're going to be a writer. So you think you can make a career of this. So you think you can publish a book. This is what you get for dreaming. This is all your dreams are worth. Five years, and the best you can do is throw it away."

My youngest son came down the stairs and I gently told him it was much too early for him to be up and walked him back to his room. When I tried handing him his favorite yellow blanket, he calmly told me that at six years old, he didn't need his blanket anymore.

I remember standing there in the shadows of our dark hallway outside his room and thinking that if he didn't need that security blanket, boy, I sure did. I stretched back out on the couch, wrapped that blanket over my legs, and sighed. If there was ever a time I needed to be positive, it was now. If there was ever a time to take comfort from my Bible, it was now.

I reached for my devotional and the suggested reading for the day was John 14. I was in no mood to read an entire chapter so I decided I would read the first verse and the last verse. The first verse said, "Let not your heart be troubled." I never realized what a sense of humor God had until then. I snickered and flipped the page to the last verse. It read, "Arise and let us go from here."

I went all right. That morning, I marched straight back to that writer's conference and asked for a refund. I was going to go back home and lick my wounds. They wouldn't give it to me, so I went to a children's fiction workshop, not willing to waste those precious dollars I had paid. Maybe I wasn't cut out for romance. Since every word I'd sold up to that point had been about my kids, maybe that was what I should be writing about.

I remember very little about that workshop except one thing.

The author Barbara Williams advised the group never to leave a rejected manuscript sitting on the desk. A few short weeks after the conference, I decided to mail that manuscript to Silhouette Books at Simon & Schuster. Yes, the same manuscript the editor told me to throw away.

AGAINST ALL ODDS

It was a gamble, I'll admit. I'd already been scorned by one editor. After almost five years all I had to show for my effort was a few dozen freelance articles. And Silhouette, the publisher to whom I was sending this manuscript, had not even responded to my letter asking permission to send the manuscript. So I'd waited, day after day, with my manuscript staring at me from the corner of my desk every time I passed, just daring me to think of myself as a writer. The moment finally came when I couldn't stand it any longer. I decided that I didn't care if the publisher wanted to see that manuscript or not; I was mailing it off.

The line at the Kent post office had never felt longer. After piling my four children into our family station wagon, there we stood, waiting my turn to hand over the package containing my finished manuscript along with my fragile hopes. Despite all the discouragement I'd received, my desire had never been stronger.

I remember it cost ten dollars to mail that manuscript: five dollars for postage and five for the return postage. For a family living on an unemployment check of $150 a week, ten dollars was no small change. As I stood there at the front of the line, praying that I was doing the right thing, a man with a kind smile behind the postal counter gently whispered, "You have to let go of the money." I unclenched my fingers and handed it over to him. I prayed all the harder as I watched my package, and my money, disappear from view.

After we got home from the post office, one of my sons raced down to the mailbox to collect the mail. Inside was a letter from Silhouette Books. In a Sharpie, the editor wrote in big letters across my neatly typed query letter: "Do not send us your manuscript: we are not buying at this time."

My heart sank. I had just wasted ten very precious dollars, and by giving in to the impulse and mailing my book off, I had actually taken something away from my children. I walked into the house, lay down on the couch, and didn't get up for the rest of the day. There was no way I would steal from my own children in order to pursue my dream. I determined then and there that my fiction-writing days were over.

It didn't matter what my practical self reasoned; I believed I was supposed to be a writer. It was my deepest desire. God knew.

Just a few weeks after sending my manuscript off I got *the* phone call. It was September 29, 1982, at 4:39 P.M. When I answered the call it was Mary Clare Susan, an editor for Silhouette Books at Simon & Schuster. Mary Clare made me an offer on the book. The very same book that the other editor had told me that no amount of rewriting would ever make sellable. The same book another editor had told me to throw away.

WE ARE ALL MEANT TO SHINE

I could have given up after the writer's conference, but something in me held on. In her book *A Return to Love*, Marianne

Williamson writes about the potentially crippling feeling of inadequacy:

> Our deepest fear is not that we are inadequate. Our deepest fear is that we are powerful beyond measure. It is our light, not our darkness, that most frightens us. We ask ourselves, Who am I to be brilliant, gorgeous, talented, fabulous? Actually, who are you *not* to be? You are a child of God. Your playing small does not serve the world. There's nothing enlightened about shrinking so that other people won't feel insecure around you. We are all meant to shine, as children do. We were born to make manifest the glory of God that is within us. It's not just in some of us; it's in everyone. And as we let our own light shine, we unconsciously give other people permission to do the same. As we're liberated from our own fear, our presence automatically liberates others.[1]

CHOOSING YOUR WORD

Having been a faithful diarist for most of my life, I'm blessed to have volumes and volumes narrating my life, year by year. It's allowed me to look back and, with the vantage point of time and distance, see how God worked in me one day at a time. Before I intentionally began to identify a word of the year, I could see that the Lord was already at work. If you retrace your steps, pay attention to the themes—the words that are repeated over and over. One of them might just be the word God chose for you.

WORDPLAY

Take a small notebook or journal and begin to gather the words that appear over and over again in your life. You might even tick off the number of times these words appear in your notes, journals, e-mails, and letters. Watch the patterns that develop. It may help you see how gently the Lord has been guiding you, one word at a time.

From My Prayer Journal

Dearest Lord, I believe so strongly in the power of dreams. All my life I felt that it was You who gave me the dream of being a writer, planting it deep within my heart, nurturing it from the time I was a child, keeping it alive in those dark years. May my words touch lives for You. Amen.

Jesus said to her, "I am the resurrection and the life. The one who believes in me will live, even though they die; and whoever lives by believing in me will never die. Do you believe this?"
—John 11:25–26

Three

BELIEVE

Be·lieve [bih-*leev*]
—verb *(used without object)* To have confidence in the truth, the existence, or the reliability of something, although without absolute proof that one is right in doing so: *Only if one believes in something can one act purposefully.*

In 1999 my word for the year was *believe.*

Across our country uncertainty and fear spread as the media began talking about the impending disaster they dubbed Y2K. As soon as the calendar page turned from 1998 to 1999, we began to hear about the disaster that awaited us in just twelve months' time. We were told that because computers had abbreviated the four-digit year to the last two digits there would be mass computer failure. Financial markets would crash. Programmable devices like VCRs, coffeemakers, and security systems would quit. Even worse would be the effects on air traffic control, hospital equipment, and nuclear weapons. Our computers would be worthless, our data lost. As the year moved forward the experts talked about food shortages, riots, and chaos. People began stocking up on food, batteries, and supplies. Even worse, gun sales skyrocketed. People even bought gas masks and radiation detectors.

On December 19 of that year I wrote in my prayer journal: "It seems not quite right to be writing about fear at this time of year. Amazing, really, with the turn of the millennium and all that goes with it—the fear and the doubt, the threat of violence and mayhem. Protect us all, Lord, and praise Your name."

As I look back I can see how I explored the word *believe* from all different angles. A large part of my reason for choosing the word was that I wanted to believe that with God's help I could lose weight. Throughout the pages of my journal and prayer journal I wrestled with this. I "claimed victory," then failed and asked forgiveness. I boldly believed and then I doubted. I decided it wasn't about weight but about belief. Then I changed my mind. In hindsight the struggle is so apparent—especially from the vantage point of having largely moved past this issue in my life. It's painful to read and yet, through it all, I never suffered a crisis of belief. If anything, that nearly lifelong struggle kept me clinging to the feet of Jesus like nothing else.

I also explored what it meant to believe all of God's promises to prosper me, to help me succeed. But most of all I concentrated on how my life had changed when I decided to follow Jesus. You may have heard me tell this story before, but because it is the hinge of my life, let me tell you how belief changed everything.

SEEDS OF BELIEF

My mother and father were godly parents. I had been raised Catholic. I regularly went to mass and attended twelve years of Catholic school in Yakima, Washington. Like my parents, I was devoted to the church. But more than that, I felt strangely drawn to God and to all things spiritual even though I had never explored the Bible or connected with Jesus Christ on a soul-deep basis.

I was the mother of two small children when, at the age of twenty-two, we moved to Seahurst, near Seattle. My neighbor Marilyn Kimmel invited me to Bible Study Fellowship. Until that point I had never set foot inside a Protestant church, but being new in the neighborhood, I was hungry for friendship. So, despite my misgivings, I packed up the toddlers and went. As soon as I pushed that door open, I had the most uncomfortable feeling. After depositing the girls in their playgroup, I tentatively joined the others, sitting on the very edge of the pew in a fight-or-flight posture. What would happen if my parents found out what I doing? No one in the Adler family had ever been disloyal to the church. I came close to leaving but just then the teaching leader got up to introduce herself. "My name is Denise Adler. . . ." Adler—my maiden name. It was as if God Himself was saying, "This is home. We are family."

That week the class was studying the first four chapters of Nehemiah. I remember Marilyn telling me somewhat apologetically that this was the year BSF was studying the minor prophets. I didn't tell her but that was okay with me, since I had no idea who was a major one! Surrounded by those dear ladies, as I starting digging into the Word it latched on to my heart. It wasn't long before I felt God tugging at me. I wanted the same relationship with Christ that my friends had. As I learned more about Him from the study and from my newfound friends and neighbors, I surrendered my life to Jesus Christ. I may be the only person you'll ever meet who came to faith while studying Nehemiah.

My friends joke that I never do things by half, so when I made the decision to follow Jesus, I knew I had to learn as much as I could to make up for the time I had lost. I got up every morning while it was still dark and spent time reading the Bible, doing devotionals, studying, and praying. I began keeping a number of journals—my personal journal, my devotional journal, my prayer journal, and a gratitude journal. I added a time at night as well so I could begin the day and close the day with Him. Those two hours are my time with God to this day and I wouldn't give it up for anything.

Developing and maintaining a relationship takes time.

BELIEVE IN THE WORD

I honestly don't think I could write the books I write if I hadn't practiced belief for forty-something years. I agree with what the writer Madeleine L'Engle had to say about it in her book *Madeleine L'Engle Herself*:

> The creative process has a lot to do with faith and nothing to do with virtue, which may explain why so many artists are far from virtuous; are, indeed, great sinners. And yet, at the moment of creation, they must have complete faith, faith in their vision, faith in their work.
>
> Again, the degree of talent, the size of their gift,

is immaterial. All artists must listen, but not all hear great symphonies, see wide canvases, conceive complex, character-filled novels. No matter, the creative act is the same, and it is an act of faith.

A ten-year-old boy asked me of *A Wrinkle in Time*, "Do you believe all that?"

"Yes," I replied. "Of course I do."

The artist, like the child, is a good believer. The depth and strength of that belief is reflected in the work; if the artist does not believe, then no one else will; no amount of technique will make the responder see truth in something the artist knows to be phony.[1]

Belief in the Face of Fear

In his book *A Grief Observed*, C. S. Lewis, while grieving the death of his wife, wrote,

> You never know how much you really believe anything until its truth or falsehood becomes a matter of life and death to you. It is easy to say you believe a rope to be strong and sound as long as you are merely using it to cord a box. But suppose you had to hang by that rope over a precipice. Wouldn't you then first discover how much you really trusted it? . . . Only a real risk tests the reality of a belief.[2]

I want to share with you a story about a woman who found belief her only lifeline when tragedy struck her. Anne Smucker was born into an Old Order Amish family in Lancaster County,

Pennsylvania. Her family traveled by horse and buggy and lived without electricity or telephone. Before she turned three the family made a change to the Amish Mennonite Church. This meant they could own a black car—no color other than black— and use electricity in the home and tractors on the farm. Cooking, baking, and caring for the family are what women in her family did, and Anne wanted to follow in their footsteps. She eventually met and married Jonas Beiler, a boy from her community. They shared their faith in God and their love of family.

Anne couldn't have been more blessed. By the time she and Jonas had been married five years in 1975, they had two beautiful little daughters, LaWonna and Angie. They had just moved into their own sixty-foot double-wide trailer on the family farm. The girls could play barefoot in the warm earth and were surrounded by family, by people who loved them. Life couldn't have been more perfect. It was easy to believe in God—to believe He had a plan for their lives.

One Sunday after church, nineteen-month-old Angie ran out the door to visit her grandmother. Anne watched her hurry off, her pale curls bouncing as they caught the sunlight. Moments later, Anne heard the sound that stopped her heart—her sister Fi's screams tangled with the anguished voice of her father, calling for her. She ran, meeting her father as he rounded the corner carrying a limp Angie.

She knew. Nothing would ever be the same again.

Fi, who worked the farm alongside her dad, always watched carefully as she used the Bobcat. She'd look behind and then turn around again just to make sure there were no pets or children nearby. Yet somehow that day Fi had backed the Bobcat over her beloved little niece. Though Angie showed no signs of outward trauma, she was gone.

As best she could Anne coped, but inside something cold had begun to grow. Depression set in and with it a crisis of faith. As Anne Beiler said in an article in the *Pentecostal Evangel*,

> Had it not been for God's grace and mercy, and the wonderful godly husband who loved me as Christ loves him, I never would have climbed out of depression. I believe Angela was sent to me and my family for many reasons, but a key purpose was for me to become the kind of person that Christ wants me to be. I experienced emotional pain, anguish of soul and deep depression as a result of her death.[3]

As the Beilers began to rebuild their lives, Jonas confessed to Anne that his dream was to open a counseling center in the Amish community in which they'd both grown up. Anne couldn't imagine where they'd come up with the money to make that happen, but she agreed to find a job to help this dream come true. With only a ninth-grade education, this was no easy feat, but she ended up working at a market stand making soft pretzels. According to Anne, those first pretzels tasted awful. The couple went to work on the recipe until they got it just right. They called it pretzel perfection. They eventually bought the stand. Before long they were selling 1,500 hand-rolled pretzels a day and Auntie Anne's Hand-Rolled Soft Pretzels was born.

Coming out of that darkness, light became more important than ever to the Beilers. Their company focused on light and they used the acronym as part of their mission statement—*L*ead by example, *I*nvest in employees, *G*ive freely, *H*onor God, *T*reat all business contacts with respect.

By the time the Beilers sold the company in 2005, there were

250 franchises that sold more than 107 million pretzels a year. And they had enough money to build Anne and Jonas's dream: the Family Center in Gap, Pennsylvania.

The Beilers know what it is to believe in God and to believe in a dream. As Anne said,

> I know where I came from, and I keep looking back to remember. I'm a country girl from the farm. I know what it's like to work hard. I've experienced plenty of pain and things in my life that have been unpleasant and I know that God is my Source. I stay focused on Him and He keeps taking me places where I'm forced to depend on Him for my every need—emotionally, spiritually and for wisdom.[4]

Anne Beiler—Auntie Anne—also knows what it is to believe despite facing both the worst imaginable tragedy and the best imaginable triumphs.

> God has a plan for our lives. We can have confidence in Him that He will take us where He wants us to go. We don't have to become fearful and wonder what God's will is. It will come to us and unfold over time. We need to trust Him for our futures. Each day we must do what is at hand and be faithful in the little things.[5]

"Trust Him for our futures." That's good advice from Anne Beiler. As my year wound to a close, I noticed that spending a year exploring belief had strengthened my faith. Trust comes easier when our faith is solid.

Choosing Your Word

Once you've chosen your word, spend the year exploring it from all angles. During 1999, I looked at my word, *believe*, in light of belief in God, belief in myself, unbelief, belief for healing from unhealthy eating patterns, belief that God did indeed hold the world in His hands despite the looming Y2K crisis, belief that God would care for my children . . . I chewed on this word for fifty-two weeks. At the end of the year all I could say is, "I do believe; help me overcome my unbelief!" (Mark 9:24).

Wordplay

As a way of sharing your word and having some artistic fun with it, why not design—or have a calligrapher or artist friend design—a greeting card to use throughout the year with your word on it? Some words won't lend themselves to this treatment, but others will make a perfect card.

From My Prayer Journal

Dearest Jesus, I know how much You love me. I've seen it each and every day of my life. I marvel at Your goodness to me and wonder why You have chosen to bless me with such abundance. My word for this year is believe—to believe in You and believe in myself. I am astonished and grateful for the way You have worked in my life. Amen.

Then Jesus declared, "I am the bread of life.
Whoever comes to me will never go hungry, and
whoever believes in me will never be thirsty."
—John 6:35

Four

HUNGER

Hun·ger [*huhng*-ger]
—noun A compelling need or desire for food. The painful
sensation or state of weakness caused by the need of food: *to
collapse from hunger.*

The year was 1979—more than thirty years ago. My word for
that year was *hunger*. It's a strange word to choose. You'd
hardly call it one perfect word, but it made sense for me, for
then.

I was attending college classes at the time—taking writing
classes among other coursework. I recently thought about that
year because two of the teachers I had from that time came to
Port Orchard to have lunch with me in the Victorian Rose Tea
Room, which Wayne and I own. We had a good visit, but seeing them reminded me how hungry I was for education and, of
course, to learn more about writing. I wanted to be a novelist so
badly I could taste it. That's hunger.

In my journal that year I wrote, "I keep thinking about writing a book. I made a suggestion in class on Wednesday. My idea was to take 1 Thessalonians and call the book *Living the Letters*. I could use anecdotes about what has happened in my life while reading 1 Thessalonians for one month. Next month I'm going to be doing Ephesians." Reading that now I have to laugh. That idea came to me thirty years before the bestselling book *The Year of Living Biblically*.

Yes, I was also hungry for more of God's Word. Thankfully it has always been an insatiable hunger. On Good Friday, I wrote in my journal: "Read through the first book of John. Only five chapters and yet I feel I'm only skimming the surface of what it means to live a Christian life. Today was the first fasting day for me, only I didn't spend the time in prayer that I had intended to. Consequently, it was a difficult day, and my mind was on my hunger."

THE OPPOSITE OF HUNGER

Yes, that kind of hunger, too. Physical hunger. Part of the reason 1979 was about hunger had to do with my nearly lifelong struggle with food. As I read over my journals, the battle with food consumes pages and pages. If I were to venture a guess, I'd say that I mention eating or food in at least half of all entries. The struggle to lose weight had become almost an obsession. Here is just a sample of entries:

> *Dearest Lord, in the area of food my struggles are legion. It is as if all my weaknesses are located in one pocketed area. I've known for a long time now that You, Lord Jesus, are my only answer, that only in You and in my faith would I find peace. I have pleaded and wept and*

You have listened and challenged, guided and loved.
Thank You for Your patience with me as I continue with
this struggle.

Dear Lord, as I struggle to gain control over my eating
habits I turn to You. Your Word promises victory. I claim
that victory in Your all-powerful name and boldly ask
You to take me by the hand and walk every step with
me. Every day I must simply take the NTS—next tiny
step—and I thank You in advance for this day, Lord, for
this victory.

I was hungry to overcome my obsession with food. I constantly dieted, winning some days, failing more than I suc-
ceeded. I was starved for healing. Paul talked about his "thorn
in the flesh" (2 Corinthians 12:6–8). My inability to control my
eating became my own thorn. In the year 2000, and with a dia-
betes diagnosis, I wrote: "My God-side is at odds each and every
day with my desire for food. I'm down thirty pounds or more
from this time a year ago. This is the struggle of my life. I'm
keenly aware that this is a battle for my very life."

When I chose that word *hunger*, little did I know that it
would be more than twenty-five years until God answered the
prayers that filled those journal pages.

HUNGER FOR PLACE

There were other hungers I explored as well. With four little
children in a tiny house, I was always hungry for more space—a
little room to spread out. Of course, I had nothing to complain
about.

When I read the story of how Temple University got its start, it made my hunger for a little elbow room seem pretty petty. Who would ever guess that fifty-seven cents and a little girl's hunger for a seat in Sunday school could change the direction of one of the leading religious, medical, and educational institutions in our country?

Hattie May Wiatt lived near Grace Baptist Temple in Philadelphia. At that time it was housed in a cramped building. Each Sunday so many people came, just trying to squeeze in to get a seat, that church members figured the only fair way was to offer admission tickets. These were handed out weeks in advance for every service. The Sunday school was just as crowded. Every Sunday, as the pastor, Reverend Russell H. Conwell, came to open the doors and usher in the children, he would always find a crowd of children who simply could not fit into the Sunday school. Hattie May was often in that crowd. One day, Rev. Conwell went to visit Hattie's family. Here's his account of that visit:

> As we met, I said: "Hattie, we are going to have a larger Sunday school room soon."
>
> "I hope you will," she said. "It is so crowded that I am afraid to go there alone."
>
> "Well," I replied, "when we get the money with which to erect a school building we are going to construct one large enough to get all the little children in, and we are going to begin very soon to raise the money for it." It was only in my mind as a kind of imaginary vision, but I wished to make conversation with the child.[1]

Hattie took his words to heart and began saving her money. Sadly, the little girl became sick and died. After her death her mother found the lumpy handmade purse that contained the pennies and the note that said, "To help build Temple Sunday School so more children can go." When she gave it to Rev. Conwell, he decided to make it the centerpiece of an effort to find enough space so that all the children could come. He took those fifty-seven cents to the congregation and told them the story of Hattie's hunger for a bit of room in which to come and learn about Jesus. He then offered the pennies for sale. In those days, at the turn of the last century, he collected an impressive $250 from the sale of those fifty-seven cents. They then took that money, changed it into pennies, and sold them for enough to buy the property next door. That was just the start.

One small girl's hunger for a little space in which to go to Sunday school not only fueled the building of a new church but also formed the seed money for Temple University's Temple University Hospital, and Temple University School of Medicine.

SEHNSUCHT: THE INCONSOLABLE LONGING

Getting back to my original thoughts on hunger . . . we think of it as a blight—and it is when people are literally starving—but when that longing comes from God, it's a powerful tool.

C. S. Lewis talked about that kind of longing in many of his writings. He used the German word *Sehnsucht* to describe it. The word has no direct translation to English—it's complex, more like craving, yearning, or yes, hunger. It's a sense of hungering for something just out of our reach—something that is familiar, only half-remembered. Lewis called it "an inconsolable longing." He saw it as that God-hunger that is in all of us. In *The Weight of Glory*, Lewis said:

In speaking of this desire for our own far-off country, which we find in ourselves even now, I feel a certain shyness. I am almost committing an indecency. I am trying to rip open the inconsolable secret in each one of you—the secret which hurts so much that you take your revenge on it by calling it names like Nostalgia and Romanticism and Adolescence; the secret also which pierces with such sweetness that when, in very intimate conversation, the mention of it becomes imminent, we grow awkward and affect to laugh at ourselves; the secret we cannot hide and cannot tell, though we desire to do both. We cannot tell it because it is a desire for something that has never actually appeared in our experience. We cannot hide it because our experience is constantly suggesting it, and we betray ourselves like lovers at the mention of a name.[2]

Lewis tries to name that indescribable feeling—that hunger we all have—for something unnamed and far-off. Some people harbor that yearning for a time or place, like pioneer days or Regency England. They say things like, "I was born in the wrong era." Some people delve into their Irish or Scottish roots and gather all things Celtic. I've met people descended from slaves who long to go back to Africa to discover a sense of self—the secret hunger C. S. Lewis talks about. He believes this yearning is really a hunger for God and for our true spiritual home. He goes on to say,

These things—the beauty, the memory of our own past—are good images of what we really desire; but if they are mistaken for the thing itself they turn into dumb idols, breaking the hearts of their worshippers. For they are not the thing itself; they are only the scent of a flower we have not found, the echo of a tune we have not heard, news from a country we have never yet visited.[3]

I spent a year exploring hunger, though I have to admit, I rarely experienced the literal kind that year. There always seems to be plenty of food, but I still have the *sehnsucht* kind of hunger—a hunger for that far-off place. And that's not a bad thing at all.

CHOOSING YOUR WORD

Sometimes you will completely understand why you chose a certain word. Other times you will be mystified. It's almost as if the word chooses you. Part of the fun of living with one perfect word for a whole year is that you can get to the very bottom of it. No, you'll never know all there is to discover, but as you dig you'll uncover layer after layer. Ask your friends what the word means to them. If you are a social media user, blog about your word, inviting comments. Collect dictionary meanings. Circle the word every time you come across it in literature or poetry. Instead of skimming over ideas as we often have to do, with your one word you can afford to go deep.

WORDPLAY

Your word may lend itself to the admonition to "taste and see" (Psalm 34:8). If I were to choose a word like *hunger* today, I might have a dinner with friends to culminate a time of fasting. Nothing tastes as wonderful as the food eaten following a fast. A discussion of hunger—all types of hunger—would help redefine the word. Another thing I might do is mount a little challenge for myself for the year. What if every time we said (or thought), "I'm hungry," we set a dollar aside for World Vision? It might help us put our word into perspective. While these ideas are specific to my chosen word for 1979, they can be adapted creatively to your word.

Dearest Jesus, it seems each day I read about people starving all across the world. This does concern me, but there are also starving people in my town, only food is not what they need. Their lack is spiritual. Six out of seven people right here in Kitsap County don't know You! That is an amazing statistic—not an encouraging one. My hope is that I have eyes to see and a heart to respond. Amen.

Blessed is the one who trusts in the Lord, *whose confidence is in him. They will be like a tree planted by the water that sends out its roots by the stream. It does not fear when heat comes; its leaves are always green. It has no worries in a year of drought and never fails to bear fruit.*
—Jeremiah 17:7–8

Five

TRUST

Trust [truhst]
—noun Reliance on the integrity, strength, ability, surety, etc. of a person or thing; confidence. Confident expectation of something; hope.
—verb To rely upon or place confidence in someone or something. To have confidence; hope.

The year was 1986 and the word I chose was *trust*. Looking back, I can see why God helped me select that word. On the first pages of my journal I talk about the worry that consumed the whole year—methane gas. Midway Landfill had never been properly prepared as a waste facility. Although our house was miles away from the landfill, the gas traveled through the porous earth until it gathered and settled in our neighborhood and in our yard, bubbling up from the ground like toxic champagne. The discovery was more than disquieting.

Wayne and I were raising our children, ranging in age from middle school to high school—four of our own and as many friends as they could manage to pack in. When we stepped outside all I could see was bubbling methane. Those neighbors with basements faced the very real danger of seeing their houses explode from built-up gas fumes. I worried. We spent many an evening attending contentious community meetings where lawyers milled around outside handing out business cards. Between neighborhood meetings and trying to take care of my family, I was at my wit's end.

And there was that word: *trust*.

We were sick that whole year. I'd just manage to get one child well when another would become ill. I don't know that I connected the toxic neighborhood with our seemingly endless illnesses, but it probably contributed to the string of sickness.

Unfortunately, as if the pressure from outside were not enough, the stress inside our home ratcheted up. Wayne and I began to experience fissures in the bedrock of our marriage. Wayne, who hates change, didn't want to move. He believed the problem would somehow right itself. He couldn't hear what I was saying or take the danger seriously.

The city of Seattle brought in a huge pumping station and set it up in the corner of our yard. Day and night the methane gas continued to bubble up out of the ground—a constant reminder of danger. It somehow became symbolic of the trouble brewing below the surface of my life.

Later, I would read Isaiah 40:31, which says, "But they that wait upon the LORD shall renew their strength." I wrote in my prayer journal:

> *Dearest Father, thank You for the reminder that You love me, You will help me live a new life in You, You will fight for me. Fight, Lord. Stand at my side in this battle,*

*for without You I am weak, but You are so incredibly
strong. Let me use Your strength. The best part, the part
that leaps off the page, is the sure knowledge that You
win. What an all-powerful promise. I look forward with
eagerness to do exactly that. Together, Father, we shall
overcome this.*

We talked about a lawsuit, but the attorneys asked for more
money than we had. How could we possibly come up with five
thousand dollars for a retainer?

Experiencing the Word from All Angles

Trust. When you choose your word, you need to be ready to
experience it from a number of different angles. That year fear
battled trust much of the time. Eventually the city of Seattle
ended up buying us out. We moved in September of that year.
Wayne remained convinced it was a mistake to leave our home.
I insisted we find somewhere else to live.

It didn't help that the new house we bought came with hidden problems like a leaky roof. When the first rain came, the
water seeped in. At the same time I was getting pressure from
my agent and publisher to write books with a heightened sensu-
ality. Financially, the only thing that kept us afloat was my nov-
elizing soap operas. I received four thousand dollars a book and
managed to write five books that year.

So God provided. The roof was patched, the methane gas became the city of Seattle's problem, and I decided to trust in the
Lord and stick to writing my "traditional" romances.

KNOWING THE VOICE WE TRUST

I found a helpful story in the second part of D. L. Moody's book *Pleasure and Profit in Bible Study and Anecdotes and Illustrations*:

> I was standing with a friend at his garden gate one evening when two little children came by. As they approached us he said to me:
>
> "Watch the difference in these two boys."
>
> Taking one of them in his arms he stood him on the gatepost, and stepping back a few feet he folded his arms and called to the little fellow to jump. In an instant the boy sprang toward him and was caught in his arms. Then turning to the second boy he tried the same experiment. But in the second case it was different. The child trembled and refused to move. My friend held out his arms and tried to induce the child to trust to his strength, but nothing could move him. At last my friend had to lift him down from the post and let him go.
>
> "What makes such a difference in the two?" I asked.
>
> My friend smiled and said, "The first is my own boy and knows me; but the other is a stranger's child whom I have never seen before."
>
> There was all the difference. My friend was equally able to prevent both from falling, but the difference was in the boys themselves. The first had assurance in his father's ability and acted upon it, while the second, although he might have believed in the ability to save him from harm, would not put his belief into action.
>
> So it is with us. We hesitate to trust ourselves to the loving One whose plans for us are far higher than any we

have ourselves made. He, too, with outstretched arms, calls us.[1]

When I first read that story I wrote this prayer in my journal: "Dear Lord, Your word says that Your sheep know You and listen to Your voice. This is my prayer for my own life. May I always be tuned to listen to Your voice. May I respond instantly like the youth in the story, with love and obedience—trusting in my Lord, my Savior, my God. Amen."

I still seek that level of trust.

STEPPING OUT IN TRUST

The word *trust* is summed up perfectly in this quote by Patrick Overton: "When you have come to the edge of all light that you know and are about to drop off into the darkness of the unknown, faith is knowing one of two things will happen: There will be something solid to stand on or you will be taught to fly."[2]

In 1956, five young missionaries taught us that trust sometimes costs more than we ever imagined.

Jim Elliot was the first of the five to hear stories about the fierce Ecuadorian tribe referred to as Auca Indians. The word *auca* actually means "savage" and was applied to the tribe as a description. The tribe's true name was the Huaorani, a name simply meaning "the people." From the days of the Spanish conquistadors until the 1950s era of oil company exploration, every single outside encounter recorded with the Huaorani ended in death. Their propensity to kill had become legendary. They not only killed their enemies but they frequently killed their own tribe members and even family.

Jim Elliot and his wife, Elisabeth, along with his college friends Nate Saint and Ed McCully and their wives, were already working as missionaries in Ecuador. They talked often of the Huaorani, feeling drawn toward these primitive people who had no written language and had never heard the story of Jesus Christ. They eventually recruited two other friends and colleagues, Peter Fleming and Roger Youderian, to mount a mission to connect with the much-feared Huaorani in what they called Operation Auca.

Nate Saint, the pilot for the group, started flying over the area inhabited by the tribe, trying to spot a suitable place where they could eventually land and make contact. He found a sandbar in the Curaray River that would work as a makeshift landing strip. They began flying over the nearby village, dropping small gifts, so that the Huaorani would become familiar with the plane. Eventually they rigged a bucket so gifts could be lowered into the waiting hands of the tribesmen. The men were delighted when the people reciprocated, sending gifts back like monkey meat and a pet parrot.

As the missionaries continued to make contact, their wives waited back at their homes, taking turns manning the radio. Between the five families there were nine small children.

On January 2, 1956, Nate Saint flew the others in, one at a time, to the camp they would call Palm Beach. They camped on the beach for three days before finally seeing two naked women step out of the jungle on the opposite side. Two of the missionaries swam over to greet the women. Soon a young man stepped out of the jungle as well. The three Huaorani seemed completely at ease and shared a meal of hamburgers and Kool-Aid with the men. The man kept pointing to the airplane, calling it *ibo*. It became obvious he wanted a ride, so Nate Saint took him up in the plane and flew him over his village. The people looked up when they heard the noise of the engine and recognized him as he waved and called. As he landed, the Huaorani left one by one. The men reported back to their wives that the day had been a success. They'd made friendly contact.

The next day they saw no Huaorani but on January 8, Nate did an overflight and saw a party of men heading their way. At noon, Nate Saint radioed his wife, Marge, to say, "Looks like they'll be here for the Sunday afternoon service. This is it! Pray for us. Will contact you again at four thirty; over and out."

A Tragic End?

The wives waited and prayed. When four thirty came with no contact they knew something was wrong. Marge Saint contacted the other missionary pilot in the area to do a check on them. The next morning the pilot flew over the camp and spotted the airplane, stripped of the canvas that once formed the plane's skin. As he flew in for a closer look he saw a body in the river. The families knew something terrible had occurred.

Four days later a rescue and recovery party reached the spot and recovered the remains of all five men. The world heard about the tragedy when *Life* magazine did a ten-page article on their mission, their lives, and their deaths. Those who read the story believed they would never know what took place that day on the beach.

A New Beginning

But there's more to the story. Nate Saint's sister, Rachel, had been living and working nearby, learning the Huao language from a young Huaorani girl, Dayuma, who had fled the tribe during an especially violent time. Less than three years after the murders, Rachel Saint and Elisabeth Elliot had made successful contact and were living and working with the tribe. Many tribe members had come to faith. Nate Saint's son, Steve, who was not quite five when his father was killed, often came to spend summers with his aunt Rachel and the Huaorani.

Steve Saint moved with his own family to Ecuador in 1995 to live with the Huaorani and help them build an airport and a hospital. In 1996 he wrote an article titled "Did They Have to Die?" in *Christianity Today,* in which he said, "Though I knew which men had killed Dad, it was not something I asked about. According to Huaorani tradition, as my father's oldest son I would primarily be responsible for avenging his death in kind." Even Steve's aunt Rachel, who'd lived with the Huaorani for thirty-seven years, had heard few details.

The Rest of the Story

One day he was sitting outside Dayuma's house with a group of Huaorani—including some of the killers who had since become believers and friends. He asked the evangelist, Dyuwi, how many times he had killed before he turned his life over to God. As they all began to share their history, the story of that day on the beach emerged. Steve Saint began to see the event from a totally different perspective.

The entire event grew out of teenage angst, a series of misunderstandings, and a tangle of lies. The young man who appeared out of the jungle that first day was Nankiwi. He had decided he wanted to take another wife and settled on the young girl who appeared first on the beach with the older woman. Her brother and mother strenuously objected. This angered Nankiwi and the girl. In what seems to us a typical teenage reaction, the young girl stomped off, saying that if she couldn't marry Nankiwi she might as well go to the *cowodi*—the foreigners—and let them kill her. Nankiwi followed her. The older woman, aware that the couple could be killed for going off together alone, followed to chaperone. That's how the three ended up meeting the missionaries.

When the men of the tribe had seen Nankiwi in the airplane, they decided they would visit as well. They set out the next morning and ran into Nankiwi and the girl heading back to the village. The older woman had stayed back at the beach. This infuriated the girl's brother and he threatened to kill Nankiwi. In order to deflect attention from himself Nankiwi said that the *cowodi* had attacked them and they were fleeing for their lives.

Most in the tribe did not trust Nankiwi's truthfulness, but tempers flared and some of the older men told stories of how deceptive and bloodthirsty outsiders were. They went back to the village to sharpen spears and collectively worked themselves into a vengeful state.

When the old woman came back and saw what was happening, she knew Nankiwi had lied. She tried to talk the men out of their killing rage but failed. Generations of distrust and fear made the attack inevitable.

The missionaries had guns but had decided long before that if attacked, they would not use them. The six Huaorani with spears knew they were no match for five outsiders with guns but they felt obligated to avenge the purported wrong.

They couldn't understand why the men didn't shoot or run into the jungle. It made no sense.

AND ANGELS SANG

Dawa, one of three women who'd accompanied them, had hidden in the bush. She heard the killings but did not see them. What she did see changed her forever. She related to Steve Saint that when the killing was finished she saw *cowodi* hovering above the trees singing. She described what we would call angels.

Two of the killers, Mincaye and Kimo, told Steve Saint they also heard the singing along the ridge above the beach. In the article Steve Saint wrote, he said, "Dyuwi verified hearing the strange music, though he describes what he saw more like lights, moving around and shining, a sky full of jungle beetles similar to fireflies with a light that is brighter and doesn't blink."

The deaths of those five young men—deaths heralded by angels and mourned by humans—inspired a whole generation. Jim Elliot's journal entry for October 28, 1949, summed up his commitment to the mission that was more important than his life: "He is no fool who gives what he cannot keep to gain that which he cannot lose."

All five—Nate Saint, Jim Elliot, Ed McCully, Peter Fleming, and Roger Youderian—stepped out into that darkness and were taught to fly, so to speak. And because they trusted God for the eternal outcome, a whole tribe will never be the same.[3]

Trust. What power is packed into that simple five-letter word!

My journal sums up the year.

> *I celebrated Thanksgiving Day with gratitude to a loving God who gave me so very much. I think back on this year and how different this has been from my expectations. There have been so many things that have brought me to my knees. I've grown closer to the Lord, and I know that He will take care of us. I have trusted You, Jesus. Thank You.*

CHOOSING YOUR WORD

When it comes to choosing your word for the year, don't shy away from words that you perceive could be "asking for trouble." I've heard people jokingly say, "Never pray for patience. It's a sure way to invite heaps of trouble." If God is calling you to explore a weighty word, like *loss* for instance, don't let fear stop you from discovering what it is God would have you learn. The blessing that will come from trusting Him and letting Him take you on a journey of discovery will far outweigh the risk. He is trustworthy.

WORDPLAY

My friend has a large stone with her word of the year cut into it. She uses it as a paperweight. She has another one she uses as a doorstop; she says, "I like to stumble over my word every now and then." Stones like these can be purchased online at www.inspirationstones.com and at other places.

From My Prayer Journal

Father, may I always be steeped in Your Word so that I might never go astray or wander off the beaten path. At times the road You lead me on is precarious and risky to the human eye but You are my guardrail, my center line, and the marker that keeps me safely on the road. Amen.

*The LORD is close to the brokenhearted and
saves those who are crushed in spirit.*
—Psalm 34:18

Six

BROKENNESS

Bro·ken·ness [*broh*-kuhn-ness]
—noun The state or quality of being broken; unevenness.
Contrition.

Harriet Beecher Stowe wrote, "When you get into a tight place and everything goes against you, till it seems as though you could not hold on a minute longer, never give up then, for that is just the place and time that the tide will turn." [1] I got into that kind of tight place in 1988. I had a house full of teens and tweens. It should have been such a happy time, but my beautiful family was unraveling at the seams. I guess it stands to reason my word for that year was *brokenness*.

No one told me there could be so much pain in raising children. Of course, no one told me there would be so much joy either. As I read through my journal entries I don't know how I got through that year. Certainly I wouldn't have without relying on Christ to see me through the darkest hours of my life. Rather than tell you about it, let me just open my journal and share a few entries.

Everything only seems to get worse. The only thing that has gotten me through the last few days has been the knowledge that there is nothing Jesus and I can't face together.

Wayne didn't phone. I've been expecting his call for two nights, and my imagination ran wild. He's on a river trip. I didn't sleep, tormented by doubts. This has been such a dreadful week. I've tried to put everything in the Lord's hands, but I keep pulling it back. Claw prints mark my life and surrender. . . . Wayne called Friday night, but it was a horrible conversation. I decided then and there that whatever was left of our marriage was dead.

This is one of those topsy-turvy emotional days that drive me loony. I wrote a short chapter. My feelings for Wayne really did matter. I keep thinking I have to face the inevitable. We aren't going to be able to save this marriage. He runs and I hibernate, and it isn't helping either of us.

Wayne didn't sleep. It's been almost two weeks since he's had a decent night's rest. He's angry, bitter, lashing out. I don't know how to help him. I feel so frustrated. I sincerely doubt that he'll go to a doctor. And he didn't sleep again. Consequently, I was awake most of the night, too.

I'm driving him to work every morning. I drive him down to the ferry and then pick him up after work, and there are days that it doesn't—it just doesn't seem worth it. As I was driving, I said, "I can't do this anymore." And I just looked at him. "You know, we just have to make a decision. Either things have to change or you're going to have to leave."

That night he came home and he was in such a happy mood after days of being just dark. Every time he walked in a room it had been like a rain cloud came in. That night he said, "I want to talk to you and the kids."

"Okay," I said. "But before you do, what are you going to say? I want to know first before you talk to the kids."

He said, "I've made my decision. I'm moving out!" He was so happy. He went and got out suitcases.

All I said was, "Okay."

This hasn't been a good year. There's been so much pain and hurt. Wayne and I've come a long ways, but I feel like I'm the one who is constantly giving in. The kids have problems, and I'm left to deal with them alone.

And that's how the year ends. Broken. Utterly broken.

So, was it a mistake to choose the word *brokenness*? No. God knew. He knew more than I did at that point. I didn't think that God could ever, ever save our marriage.

But I don't want to get ahead of myself.

Broken Heroes

Someone who became an American icon also discovered the depths of brokenness.

When the flashlight finally gave out, the infamous Nickajack cave was plunged into darkness. But it was like no other darkness he'd ever known. The complete, utter absence of light deep in the belly of the cave almost smothered him. The air felt heavy, close, stifling. He had no idea how far into the cave he'd gone, but he thought that if he crawled in far enough, he'd never be able to find his way back out, and nobody would be able to locate him until after he was dead. Curled up in a fetal position, he rubbed his knees with his hands. They felt numb from the cold and from his having crawled on his hands and knees in the tight tunnels and caverns for hours. He'd half expected to come across a body of one of the many spelunkers who had died somewhere deep inside the Nickajack and had never been recovered. But no. It was just him. The loneliness hit him, heavier than the weight of the darkness. The surprise of feeling something other than despair and the lingering high of amphetamines struck him.

Johnny Cash, the beloved country singer with the unforgettable, deep baritone voice, had hit rock bottom, both literally and figuratively. As he was to say later, "The absolute lack of light was appropriate, for at that moment I was as far from God as I have ever been. My separation from Him, the deepest and most ravaging of the various kinds of loneliness I'd felt over the years, seemed finally complete."

Cash swallowed his very first amphetamine while he was touring in 1957. A doctor told him he needed something to keep him going. The nights spent performing and days back on the road were physically grueling. I understand that feeling. There have been times, touring for the release of a new book, when I didn't finish signing books and meeting readers until ten or eleven at night. Then I had to find some dinner, head back to the hotel, and leave a wake-up call for three in the morning to catch a plane to the next town. But my tours only covered weeks. Johnny Cash toured for months.

In 1967, by the time Johnny decided to end it all in Nickajack Cave, he had abused his body with addictions, uppers to keep going and downers to sleep and then uppers again to restore his energy. He had been unfaithful to his wife, injuring nearly everyone he loved in the process. He decided the world would be a better place if he crawled into a cave and never came out.

But God had other plans for Johnny Cash.

As he lay there, his mind became clearer and clearer. No matter how bad his life had been, he had never lost faith in God. How had he come to the place where he decided to take his own life? Johnny Cash wasn't the one in charge—God was. Right then he asked God's forgiveness and decided to somehow crawl back out of that cave. That was easier said than done. It was disorienting, pitch-black with a maze of tunnels honeycombing in all directions. Johnny Cash began crawling aimlessly. At one point he sensed the air stirring ever so slightly. Did he only imagine it? No. A little farther on he felt a slight breeze and followed it all the way to the cave opening.

That time in the cave changed Johnny Cash forever. It was a come-to-Jesus moment in every sense of the term. He always admitted he was the biggest sinner of all. And he knew if *he* had been forgiven, despite his broken body and spirit, anyone could be forgiven. His ministry in prisons became legendary and his career continued to grow.[2]

FLAWED BUT FIT FOR GOD'S WORK

I discovered another story of a person who experienced personal weakness and yet did great work for God.

William Carey has been called the father of modern missions. By any account, he's a fascinating, complicated character. Born in 1761 in an obscure rural village in England into a poor parish clerk's family, he never even attended the equivalent of high school, let alone college. Yet in his lifetime he translated the complete Bible into six languages and portions of it into twenty-nine others. At the age of twelve, Carey taught himself Latin. Later, on his own, he learned Greek, Hebrew, French, and Dutch. During his life he mastered dozens more languages and dialects.

He preached one of the greatest sermons of all time, "Expect Great Things, Attempt Great Things," and yet his written English was so lacking that one of his friends wrote, "I never knew a person of so much knowledge as you profess in other languages to write English so bad."

As a young man he apprenticed himself to a shoemaker, eventually taking over the business upon the man's death. He married at the age of twenty. His wife, Dorothy, was seven years his senior. It was an unlikely match for a man who loved learning, since she was illiterate. She signed her marriage license with an X. They were poor but Dorothy didn't seem to mind. Three sons were born one right after the other—Felix, William, and Peter. They'd also had two daughters but lost them both. William was a cobbler and they lived close to Dorothy's family. She was widely acknowledged to be a "home bird."

William Carey the cobbler started preaching. He became pastor of a small church, supplementing his income by teaching and mending shoes, but the family always lived on the edge of poverty.

His hunger for learning was insatiable. He devoured books. He would never be the same after reading Captain James Cook's travel journals. Carey felt called to travel to the very ends of the earth to take God's Word to those who'd never heard it.

This was long before missions were common. He became an embarrassment to many of his colleagues, but he persisted, helping to start a small missionary society. All the while Dolly, as he called his wife, stayed home tending to the boys, cooking, mending, making ends meet, and visiting with her family.

The day her husband came home from a missionary meeting and announced they were going to pack up and sail to India, her life turned upside down. She'd had no clue. In fact—according to the minutes of the meeting at which he volunteered—one of his colleagues, John Thomas, asked the society to sponsor him to Bengal, where he'd previously worked for the East India Company. They agreed. Someone turned to Carey and asked, "Will you go?" The record states: "He readily answered in the affirmative." Just like that. The society set a date for the two families to sail just three months from the meeting. He had the sailing information before he even came home to speak with his pregnant wife.

Carey's father told him he was simply mad. The society had no money with which to send him. His church objected to his leaving. And Dolly flatly refused to go. And yet, against all advice and common sense, William decided to go and take his oldest son, Felix, with him.

He set sail but had to return before he got far. His return gave him the opportunity to put pressure on Dolly, who'd given birth by this time. When he told her she could bring her sister she finally gave in. The whole family set sail—Carey enthusiastic, the rest reluctant.

When they arrived in Calcutta it soon became apparent that they had miscalculated how much it would cost them to live.

John Thomas soon abandoned the venture and reestablished his lucrative surgery, moving into upscale lodgings.

Carey had to move his family five times, trying to secure rent-free lodgings. Each one was worse than the last, malaria filled and crime ridden. Dolly and Felix battled dysentery. During this time, Carey began his Bengali language studies, working long into each night. Dolly and her sister complained bitterly but managed the best they could, suffering poverty, illness, and loneliness. It was a terrible start.

Within a year Dolly's sister, Kitty, met and married an official of the East India Company, moving away and escaping the grinding poverty. Five-year-old Peter died of dysentery just about the time Dolly found out she was pregnant again. It was too much. Her grip on sanity broke. Today her diagnosis would have been called delusional disorder, what used to be called paranoia. She believed her husband was unfaithful and followed him everywhere, accusing him in front of his colleagues, the Bengali people, and their own children. She made several attempts on his life. Eventually she had to be confined.

If that broken relationship were not painful enough, the Carey boys were out of control. Because of their mother's illness, they'd had to fend for themselves. Their father was caught up in his increasingly successful work, and by all accounts, the boys ran wild. A colleague wrote, "The good man saw and lamented the evil, but was too mild to apply an effectual remedy."

In telling this story, I've written about the brokenness, but that's only part of the story. Carey persevered, translating the Bible at a furious pace into language after language. He wasn't satisfied just creating a Bible in each dialect; he set about seeing that the people learned to read it. Along with his colleagues, he founded Serampore College, the first Christian college in Asia. Their team opened 103 mission schools. He remained sensitive and respectful of the culture, never trying to make his converts into an Indian version of the Englishman. He helped change the practice of *satī*—burning a widow on her husband's funeral pyre. His writings and his work motivated many to consider the world a "field ripe to harvest." In all, he worked in India forty-one years without a furlough.[3]

So out of such brokenness, a mighty movement was born.

RECYCLING BROKEN PIECES

The Bible often talks about pottery, comparing us to the pot and God to the potter. It's a great metaphor because so much of the work of the potter—molding, shaping, and firing—is like the work God does in our lives.

We've all dropped a plate or a piece of pottery. Once it's broken there's no putting it back together again. It will certainly not hold water even if it is mended. But did you know that for the potter, broken pieces of fired pots are recycled?

All is not lost when a pot is broken. The broken pieces of pottery are ground up and added to weak clay—clay that is too elastic. They call the pulverized shards of pottery *grog*. When the grog is added to the slumping clay, it gives strength. Interesting concept, isn't it?

Broken pieces being ground into grog and added to soft clay to build an even stronger pot is what restoration is all about. The bigger the vessel, the more grog it needs for strength. I've watched people endure incredible trials, and yet, when they come out on the other side, they insist they wouldn't change the experience. They understand they are different, far stronger, with their broken pieces making up their new vessel.

That's an image to remember: our broken pieces strengthen

us to become even bigger, stronger vessels. When I read about the "heroes" of the Bible, I'm encouraged to realize that those who were most flawed were the same ones God commended and used mightily. I'm so grateful that God didn't sanitize the Scriptures and portray the likes of Peter, David, Moses, and Abraham as near-perfect saints. We see them warts and all. The same with William Carey. He failed in caring for his family and yet he was in the vanguard of a great movement. Through him, God spoke to a nation.

Doesn't it give us hope?

CHOOSING YOUR WORD

Sometimes a word will not let you alone—like my word *brokenness*. Who would want to spend a whole year exploring something as depressing as that? I'm an optimist by nature, but I've discovered over the years that some of the most profound lessons of life have grown out of pain and struggle. I've learned—no, scratch that; I'm *learning*, when struggle comes, to lean into it and discover all I can from it. If the Lord seems to be whispering a word that you'd much rather not even think about, I encourage you to embrace it. And prepare for a year of discovery and growth. God will bless your willingness to trust Him for your word.

Wordplay

Sometimes we need to feel our word, see it, or even hear it to keep reminding us. We all have different learning modalities. If you are tactile, meaning you learn things best by touching, why not find a symbol of your word and carry it with you? I've always admired the much-rubbed worry stones some people carry with them. And I've been drawn to Charles Lutwidge Dodgson's practice of White Stone Days. You may know him by his pen name, Lewis Carroll, the author of *Alice in Wonderland*. When Carroll had a particularly memorable day he would note it in his journal as a "White Stone Day" and he'd take a smooth white stone and add it to the stones in a very large clear jar. What a visual! At the end of his life he could look at the considerable pile of stones in his jar and think back on each wonderful day. What a perfect visual and tactile reminder. If I were to choose a reminder of, say, brokenness, I might find a fragment of old flow blue pottery and tuck it deep in my pocket or purse every day. Each time my hand closed around it, I'd be reminded.

From My Prayer Journal

Dearest Jesus, many of the difficult and pain-filled periods of my life were really a training ground. When Wayne and I were separated, that was the time I fell on my knees and turned to You in prayer. By turning to You to get me through this emotionally painful time I was able to see my own part in the near-divorce and forgive Wayne his. Keeping our marriage together rerouted the entire course of my life. I'm grateful. So very grateful. Amen.

*Rejoice always, pray continually, give
thanks in all circumstances; for this is
God's will for you in Christ Jesus.*
—1 Thessalonians 5:16–18

Seven

PRAYER

Prayer [prair]
—noun A devout petition to God or an object of worship. A spiritual communion with God or an object of worship, as in supplication, thanksgiving, adoration, or confession. The act or practice of praying to God.

In 1990, my word for the year was *prayer*. It was a perfect word for a pivotal year. Wayne and I were separated and completing all the legal requirements for our divorce. Our children were suffering. I was angry. Lonely. Feeling like a failure. Resigned.

I committed to praying one hour each day that year. One whole hour. I didn't know how I'd do it when I made the promise. An hour is a very long time. Sixty slowly ticking minutes.

I prayed in our bedroom beside my bed. I would still get up very early in the morning to do my Bible reading, but now, when I was finished, I would go in the bedroom, close the door, get down on my knees, and pray. And I was there for an hour. I don't even want to confess how many times my prayer those first days was punctuated with requests for knee pain relief. When I got up I would be stiff with achy breaky knees. I literally had to train my knees to stay in that position that long.

A year ago I had a knee replacement. My son Dale said, "Mom, I'm afraid I'm responsible for that knee—all the years you spent praying for me." We laughed, but the work done on my knees over the years changed me and hopefully changed others as well. How many times have you seen the saying "Prayer changes things" cross-stitched on a wall hanging, featured on a poster, or printed on a bumper sticker? The saying is certainly true, but what's even more profound is that prayer changes us. Prayer certainly changed me.

Here's how I opened my journal in 1990:

A whole new decade stretches before me filled with promise. I feel so battle weary from the last three years of the 80s that I stand at the door of the 90s with my knees knocking. I choose to believe that God has wonderful things in store for me and my children. I've written out my goals. The kids and I did that together on the 31st. But my life belongs to Jesus. He will not abandon me. After all that's happened, it's difficult to remember that my life has been ordered by God. But I do believe this: 1990 is going to be a year of transition for me. A good year. A growth year, both spiritually and emotionally. Thank You, Jesus, for today and each day that follows.

Wayne was gone. He had moved to Nevada, and I was getting on with my life.

I remember attending a workshop called "Living, Forgiving." It was the most spiritually uplifting day of my Christian life. I came home so aware of God's love for me and for the wonderful, limitless freedom I have in Him. I wrote: "Why am I surprised at how the Lord's love surrounded me again? Wayne phoned this morning and wants reconciliation. I have serious doubts, but God is a miracle worker. I'm not even on the ways and means committee."

Later I wrote: "I've decided to go ahead with the divorce, pay Wayne his half of the assets, bury the past, and if we manage to make something of this, it would be a fresh start. I talked to Wayne for over an hour. I hate the thought of what my phone bill is going to be."

With all those hours of prayer, I now find it interesting that I didn't pray for God to heal my marriage. The divorce was set. I was ready to get on with my life. I was prepared to walk out of the marriage. I prayed that Wayne would find happiness. That he would find peace. That he would be able to make a new life for himself without bitterness and animosity.

But God knew.

Wayne called again and said, "This divorce is not working for me." He exasperated me. He was the one who'd moved out and now, just when I'd relinquished it all and was prepared to move on with my life, he wanted a reconciliation?

God had obviously been changing both of us. For me to even consider rebuilding our marriage was a sign that God had been working on me as well.

I prayed. Hard. We decided to take it slow. We "dated" for six months before making any moves, but when the time came, we made a pact. Wayne insisted. If we were to commit to marriage it would be forever; otherwise the threat of divorce would always hang over our heads. Wayne was wise in that. In all the years since, it's never been an option. We may get upset with each other, but we know we better make things right because we're in it for the long haul. We'll celebrate forty-four years of marriage soon.

THE GREATER WORK

I read that Martin Luther would pray an hour every day. But if he had an especially busy day, he'd pray for two. I can understand that, even though it's counterintuitive. That's because it's one of the lies Satan tells us—that we don't have time for prayer. That our day is too busy. That we need to just get into action. As John Wesley said, "Prayer is where the action is."[1]

The Guideposts organization has invested significant resources—both financial and organizational—in prayer and praying for the needs of the people. They man prayer hotlines. These were set up to honor the memory of Ruth Stafford Peale. Contributors have occasionally questioned this expense. Is it money wisely spent? I believe it is. Oswald Chambers once said, "Prayer does not fit us for the greater work; prayer is the greater work."[2]

HEAVEN-SENT MEATLOAF

I heard a wonderful true story about prayer from Sandra Aldrich, a speaker and writer. She first heard it from Kay Lewis. Kay heard it at Bible camp years ago from Reverend Joe Temple— they called him Brother Joe—who lived the story.

Years ago a young couple was studying at a seminary. He was preparing to be a pastor and she was taking classes in how to be a good pastor's wife in addition to working a part-time job that paid for their schooling and simple apartment. By the time they paid all their bills each month, little was left for food. So they ate a lot of oatmeal—usually three times a day.

One afternoon, the young husband came home from class with a letter he had received via the campus post office. It was from his favorite former Bible teacher who was now traveling as an evangelist. The man said he would be back in that area soon and wanted to stop by and have dinner with the student and his bride and hear how God was working in their lives. The student checked the date and realized the letter had been delayed. His former teacher would be arriving the next day! They couldn't afford a phone, so they couldn't call him. The young husband started to panic.

"We can't serve him oatmeal," he said. "What are we going to do?"

Then he took a deep breath. "Wait. We studied about impossible situations in class. We're supposed to pray."

So they bowed their heads, and the husband prayed, "Lord, I know it's prideful but we can't serve this godly man oatmeal. And we can't afford anything more than that. So we ask You to provide a good meal for him in Your creative way. In Jesus' name. Amen."

At the husband's amen, he turned to his wife. "If you could serve company anything you wanted, what would it be?"

The young wife smiled. "Oh, I have Mama's meatloaf recipe. I'd serve that."

The husband ran his hand across his mouth. "Meatloaf? Ohh!" He grabbed pencil and paper. "What all would you need for that?"

The wife thought for a moment. "Well, I'd start with two pounds of hamburger." The husband wrote that on his list. The wife continued: "Then I'd add chopped onion and two eggs. And oatmeal for a binder, but we already have that. And if we could have catsup for the top, that'd make it look pretty and would taste good, too."

The husband repeatedly wiped his mouth as he wrote the ingredients. "Oh, that's good. What would you serve with it?"

"Baked potatoes," she answered. "With sour cream and butter. And green beans. Mama used to grow the best pole beans, I think they were called 'Kentucky Wonders.' And strawberries are in season now. Strawberries and cream would make a good dessert. And coffee. We'd need coffee."

The husband's stomach growled as he placed his hands on the completed list. "Well, Lord, here's what we're asking You to provide for tomorrow's dinner. We don't know how You are going to do this, but we trust You. Amen!"

Then he turned to his wife. "When do you need these things to be here?"

She thought for a moment. "Well, I get in from work about 1:30. If I can have everything no later than 2:30, I can have it ready by the time he arrives at 6:00." Then she went into their tiny kitchen to set the table for tomorrow night's dinner.

The next day, the husband rushed into their apartment at 4:30 from his final class. Suddenly he stopped and took a deep breath. He could smell meat cooking! He hurried into the kitchen to embrace his wife. "What happened?" he asked.

She opened the oven to show him the meatloaf positioned next to three large baking potatoes. "At 2:20, somebody knocked at the door," she said. "But when I answered, nobody was there. Just a box filled with everything we had asked for."

She lifted the lid from the pan on the top of the stove. "Look at these beans," she said. "And the prettiest strawberries are waiting in the refrigerator."

Well, they had a lovely dinner that night with the former professor, and this experience became their family faith story. In the years ahead, whenever they faced tough times, they would remind each other of when God had provided that wonderful meal.

The young husband graduated, became a pastor, and eventually took on the role of a traveling evangelist—just like his former professor. One of his trips took him back to the town where the seminary was located. As he spoke one night at a local church, he told the story of God's dinner provision. He saw an elderly woman in the third row look startled, but he didn't think much about it until she greeted him after the service.

"Thank you for telling that story about the meatloaf," she said. "Because you have cleared up something that has bothered me for years."

Of course, the preacher was surprised. The woman continued. "You don't remember me," she said. "But my husband and I owned the little grocery store where you and your wife used to buy oatmeal. Only oatmeal. We wanted to help you, but every time we prayed about you, it was just as though the Lord was saying, 'Not yet.' Then one morning, I knew the Lord was saying, 'Today's the day!' Well, I couldn't wait to get to the store. Fresh vegetables had just arrived that morning so I grabbed a box and picked up two of the largest baking potatoes I'd ever seen. And the Lord said, 'Get three.' So I put that third potato in the box along with sour cream and butter. Then I placed three handfuls of the prettiest long green beans in the box—I think they were called Kentucky Wonders. And I just knew I was supposed to include the beautiful new season strawberries. Cream, too. And coffee. Then I went over to the meat case and started to pull out the biggest steaks we had. But the Lord said, 'No.' So I put my hands on the roast and heard within my spirit the same 'No.' I put my hands on the pork chops. Same thought. Finally, I plopped my hand on the hamburger. The Lord said, 'You got it. Two pounds.' "

The old woman took the preacher's hands in hers. "Now I understand."

We're missing out. Prayer is so powerful. If we could only grasp the potential that is available to us. As E. M. Bounds once said, "No learning can make up for the failure to pray. No earnestness, no diligence, no study, no gifts will supply its lack."[3]

RELATIONSHIP-BUILDING PRAYER

Prayer isn't a sacrifice. That's another lie Satan tells us. We're giving up something. Not true. We're gaining something priceless, and that is communication with our Father.

Many times our prayers are just quick arrow prayers—to the point. I'm as guilty of this as anybody else. You know the kind I mean: "Lord, find me a parking place," or "Bless that person, Lord." Or if I'm standing in line, I'll say a quick prayer for somebody ahead of me. I think it's what the Lord meant when He told us to "pray without ceasing." But those quick petitions are not the kind of prayer I'm talking about. There is nothing wrong with them. It's a natural way to communicate with your Father, but it is not relationship-building prayer. The kind of prayer I'm talking about takes time. Time to pour out our hearts and time to listen for the answer. It's real communication. If all the talk in one of our relationships were one-sided, it would be a sign that something was wrong in the relationship. Communication is a two-way street.

Since I also write down a prayer each day—in addition to the on-my-knees prayer—I am able to reread my prayers. I blushed to realize how many of my prayers were "Lord, do this. Lord, do that. Please hear me as I pray for this person." So I made it a point to start out every month with deep praise of who God is. On the first of each month I would write a version of the following:

Thank You, Father, for another incredible month and for all that it will hold. May each and every day be spent in the light of Your love as an obedient child. Make all my paths straight. From the very bottom of my heart, I thank

*You and I praise You, Father God. In some ways, I feel
like this country, this time, is on the very brink of disaster. All is bleak and yet I know that You hold the future.
You rule this world, as corrupt as it may be. You're my
God, my Father. I count on You. From when the sun
rises until it sets, I praise You. You have gifted me with
a happy, good life. I'm putting myself in Your hands that
You will take me just as I am and shape me into the
woman You have always wanted and knew I could be.*

This practice helps me mark the new month with a fresh
commitment to praise and gratitude.

My year of prayer changed me forever. I've never changed
that habit of prayer that started with my choosing one perfect
word for 1990. I can't get down on my knees any longer—for
some reason the medical community has not yet perfected an
artificial knee with that capability—but I do spend an hour with
the Lord every day. And if my day is going to be especially crazy,
I try for two.

~~Prayer changes things.~~ Prayer changes me.

CHOOSING YOUR WORD

When you've chosen your word, commit to acting on that word
as well as discovering more about the word. "Do not merely
listen to the word, and so deceive yourselves. Do what it says"
(James 1:22). For instance, if *prayer* was your word for the year,
why not commit to a prayer plan for the year—almost an experi-
ment of sorts? It's true that some words won't lend themselves
to action. For instance, if you chose to explore *death* or *loss*, you

won't necessarily want to act on those words. You'd probably want to explore the concepts. But most words don't come alive until we act on them.

WORDPLAY

My friend gave me a silver charm bracelet with many of my words engraved on hand-tooled disks. When I wear it, it is a reminder of the lessons I've learned over the years. Jesus said, "Do you have eyes but fail to see, and ears but fail to hear? And don't you remember?" (Mark 8:18). I don't want to forget all I've explored with the Lord. Tangible reminders, like my bracelet, become meaningful symbols of my walk with the Lord. Mine was handmade by the artists at Bonbon Charms, www.bonboncharms.com.

Dearest Lord, this summer has been so hectic and so full of travel that my prayer life has fallen short. I've missed those times with You, Lord, and my life has shown it. My children and grandchildren have suffered. We always hear it said, prayer changes things, but in truth, prayer changes me—it opens my eyes and softens my heart toward God, my Father. Amen.

But if anyone obeys his word, love for God is truly made complete in them. This is how we know we are in him.

—1 John 2:5

Eight

OBEDIENCE

O·be·di·ence [oh-*bee*-dee-uhns]
—noun The state or quality of being obedient. The act or practice of obeying; dutiful or submissive compliance: *Military service demands obedience from its members.* A sphere of authority or jurisdiction, especially ecclesiastical.

In 1998, I chose the word *obedience*. It's a concept I've struggled with since my earliest steps on this journey with God.

Carole Lewis, director of the Houston-based organization First Place 4 Health, says that God's love language is obedience. Obedience. Ouch! We'd like to think it would be grand gestures, impressive sacrifices, eloquent speeches, or any number of remarkable acts. Nope. It's obedience.

Teresa of Ávila said, "I know the power obedience has of making things easy which seem impossible."[1] Somehow we don't think of obedience as powerful. It seems submissive, passive. When I chose this word, I had a lot to learn about it.

Throughout the year I continued to explore the idea of obedience, especially in the area of my food obsessions. I'm sure my weight struggle was at the bottom of my choosing the word *obedience*. My prayer journal that year is like a tug of war—obedience, disobedience, good day, bad day. Was that what obedience was about? I knew I had to get off the merry-go-round of connecting my eating habits to my relationship with God. Obedience was so much more than whether or not I refrained from eating a piece of cake. Yes, God wanted me to be healthy, but as I pleaded with Him over my weight, He seemed to be telling me to wait. He wasn't taking that burden away from me just yet.

But when he did remove that lifelong obsession with food, it came in such an unusual way. All my life I believed that my struggle with weight was a spiritual problem—a shameful failing. If I were just more obedient . . . if I just had enough faith . . . if I just turned my food obsession over to God . . . if I just claimed healing . . . if I just . . . if I just . . . if I just . . . In my book *God's Guest List* I describe how I eventually had weight-loss surgery in 2005. Some might think I took a shortcut, but I've never felt God's presence so clearly in a decision. It was as if He was saying, "Enough already."

All my life I felt my weight problem could only be solved by willpower and obedience. But that wasn't what the Lord planned for me. Instead of obedience, for me it was a matter of surrender. It's not a magical cure, it still takes discipline and focus, but it was a tool to help me get past what had become an insurmountable roadblock.

The funny thing is that once the roadblock was removed, instead of my agonizing over the number on the scale each week, God showed me all kinds of other areas that needed attention. I still struggle with obedience, it's just in once-neglected areas of my spiritual life.

So how does one obey? What do we obey? I realized before I can obey the rules, I need to know the rules. The more time I spent with the Lord, with His Word, the more I understood what I was expected to do. I even had a checklist, and it wasn't long. It boiled down to two main "rules" found in Luke 10:27: " 'Love the Lord your God with all your heart and with all your soul and with all your strength and with all your mind,' " and " 'Love your neighbor as yourself.' " The Ten Commandments, the law of the Old Testament—all that can be boiled down to those two commandments.

Apart from the rules, there's one other aspect to obedience, and that's responding to the nudges. When I get those uncomfortable nudges—like I ought to call someone I've inadvertently wronged or I should take a casserole to a grieving family—I need to learn to recognize God's voice. The more we practice listening to His voice and acting on it, the better we get at recognizing it.

OBEDIENCE VS. DISOBEDIENCE

Obedience comes with promises as well. Deuteronomy 11:26–28 says we will be blessed if we obey. Unfortunately, the flip side of that passage is that we are cursed when we disobey. Job 36:11–12 tells us that if we obey we will spend the rest of our days in prosperity. Of course it also says if we disobey we will die by the sword and die without knowledge. Notice the duality of it. If you obey, something good happens. If you don't, something bad happens.

Is it a form of holy blackmail?

No. God is telling us about the natural consequences of obedience vs. disobedience. It's just as we taught our children: "If you stay close to me, you won't get lost, but if you wander you could get lost or worse." Or "If you eat your vegetables you'll grow up strong and healthy, but if all you eat is candy, your teeth will rot." We were not trying to blackmail our children. We were simply stating a fact—a natural consequence.

God says in Exodus 15:26 that if we listen carefully to what God says and obey Him, we will have none of the diseases He brought on the Egyptians. It makes sense. If we obey Him we are living worry-free, eating healthy food, and caring for each other. It is natural that we will avoid a whole host of diseases— heart disease, gout, anxiety, and any number of illnesses. Here's the most important thing I learned: God's rules are not restrictive, they are freeing.

OBEDIENCE AS A PREREQUISITE TO EFFECTIVE PRAYER

I've learned that obedience and prayer are not interchangeable. A. W. Tozer said it well:

> Have you ever noticed how much praying for revival has been going on of late—and how little real revival has resulted? I believe the problem is that we have substituted praying for obeying and it simply won't work. To pray for revival while ignoring the plain precept laid down in scripture is to waste a lot of words and get nothing for your trouble. Prayer will become effective when we stop using it as a substitute for obedience.[2]

I heard a great account of a woman's experience with prayer and obedience. Debra K. Matthews tells this story:

Winter had arrived and I needed studded tires for my van. As hard as I tried, though, I just didn't have any extra money to put away for them.

The Lord had provided so many things in my life, often just in the nick of time, that I was surprised He wasn't providing in this case. "Lord," I complained one day, "I don't understand what's wrong. You know I can't drive on the slick roads. I can walk to and from work, but it will be late at night when I get off, and it's not safe walking that far. I can't seem to do anything by myself to get enough extra money."

I worked in a retail toy store that sold at discount prices, and they naturally couldn't pay high wages. I was barely getting by. I prayed and "complained" for a few minutes before the Lord could get me to listen. Then I heard the still small voice.

"I'm always faithful to do My part, when My people are faithful to do their part," He said, and a "picture" of a situation at work flashed in my mind.

Ouch! It was like when a father gives that certain look to a child who's acting up—the child knows just exactly what that look means. I knew instantly what the Lord was trying to tell me and where I had failed.

"I'm sorry, Lord. I haven't been a very good example, have I?"

I went to work that Saturday, and trusted the Lord to bring a certain person to me while I was counting money from the previous day's sales. Throughout the day, managers and assistant managers came into the locked safe room where I was working, with each hour's money drop. Finally, in the early afternoon, the particular assistant the Lord was dealing with me about came on duty and her turn came to make the drop.

"I owe you an apology," I said to her after she'd locked the safe.

"What do you mean?" she asked me, surprised.

"Well, I got in trouble last night with the big boss," I said, smiling and pointing upward.

She laughed. She was an admitted agnostic, and we'd had plenty of conversations about the Lord over the past few months. I'd told her about Him being so real in my life, and my very dearest friend, and what the Bible says about man outside of God. She'd said she was searching, but as an intellectual, she had a real hard time accepting that there was this big, unseen God out there somewhere.

"I was sort of complaining about a certain need in my life not being met. I didn't hear an 'audible' voice with my physical ears, but just as clear as could be, the Lord spoke to my heart and said, 'I'm always faithful to do My part, when My people are faithful to do their part.'

"At the same time, I had a picture come to my mind of the way I've been here at work lately."

I felt a little sheepish, and probably looked it as I said, "I've been telling you all about the good things God has done in my life, and how He's been such a good provider and everything. But lately, I've been sort of caught up in the general conversations around here about the 'discount wages' and stuff like that. I've done a lot of 'grumbling' myself, when I know better. God said He would take care of me, and He always has.

"Anyway, I haven't been a very good example of a Christian, and I apologize," I finished.

She didn't know what to think about that. I got the impression that her past experience with Christians seemed like they were know-it-alls. To have one apologizing to her seemed surprising. We talked some more and then she headed back out to the sales floor.

After work that night, I got a call from my mom. "Have you bought studded tires for the van yet?" she asked. She knew I always put studs on my vehicles, and this was my first winter with the van, a vehicle much larger than I'd owned before.

"Not yet," I answered. "Why do you ask?"

"Well, one of the gals gave me a pair of studded tires," she said. "They're too big for our cars, so I thought about the van."

I don't remember why she said they had an extra set of tires, but they were like new, and the exact size I needed. The Lord had just been waiting for me to be obedient in a situation where I hadn't, and then He provided miraculously again!

And besides that, it gave me something else neat to tell the assistant manager about the next time we spoke![3]

I had to laugh when I read that story. It reminds me of the way God speaks to me. Henry Blackaby wrote, "God's commands are designed to guide you to life's very best. You will not obey Him if you do not believe Him and trust Him. You cannot believe Him if you do not love Him. You cannot love Him unless you know Him."[4]

To receive God's very best, we need to obey Him. In this age of free spirits, obedience has fallen into disfavor. How many of today's couples remove the promise to obey from their wedding vows? Many modern parents don't even require obedience from their children. They choose instead to run their families as some sort of benign democracy where children and parents alike are consulted and every situation results in a mutually acceptable compromise. I won't even comment. Suffice it to say that if obedience is important to God for His children, it's equally important as we parent our children.

BLIND OBEDIENCE

The hardest part of obedience for most of us is blind obedience—obeying before we've had a chance to intellectually buy in to the action. A while ago I came across this story that illustrates the importance of blind obedience:

> In July 1976, Israeli commandos made a daring raid at an airport in Entebbe, Uganda, in which 103 Jewish hostages were freed. In less than fifteen minutes, the soldiers had killed all seven of the kidnappers and set the captives free.
>
> As successful as the rescue was, however, three of the hostages were killed during the raid. As the commandos entered the terminal, they shouted in Hebrew and English, "Get down! Crawl!" The Jewish hostages understood and lay down on the floor, while the guerrillas, who spoke neither Hebrew nor English, were left standing. Quickly the rescuers shot the upright kidnappers.
>
> But two of the hostages hesitated—perhaps to see what was happening—and were also cut down. One young man was lying down and actually stood up when the commandos entered the airport. He, too, was shot

with the bullets meant for the enemy. Had these three heeded the soldiers' command they would have been freed with the rest of the captives.[5]

The problem with blind obedience is that it requires trust. We need to learn that we can trust the Lord. If He gives a command, lays down a precept, or whispers a nudge, we need to trust that it is meant for our good. We also need to recognize that if we ignore His rules, there will be consequences.

CHOOSING YOUR WORD

When you've chosen your word, make an exhaustive study of the word. Check out the definition. It might be fun to see if you can find a commentary that explains the Greek or Hebrew origin. Note how the word has been used in literature and even how the word has evolved over the years. Has it changed in meaning and acceptance? Take my word *obedience*. It is key to the Christian faith and yet both *submission* and *obedience* have fallen out of favor in our culture—linked with social dominance, abuse, and slavery. The real meaning and the blessing that goes hand in hand with the word have been lost. Ask yourself if your word needs to be redeemed and plucked out of social disfavor before you can begin to get to the bottom of what it means.

WORDPLAY

My friend is having stepping stones made of each one of her words to be used in her garden. She believes it will make the path all the more meaningful. And again, it creates a tangible reminder of our walk with the Lord. Custom stones can be ordered from www.etchedcreations.biz.

From My Prayer Journal

Dearest Lord, everyday obedience is what I long for— such simplicity—and with that obedience everything in my life falls into place. I'll follow, Jesus. Lead me, Lord. Take me wherever You wish. Guide me. Take my hand in Yours. Guard my steps. Show me the way and keep me safe from harm. I love You, Lord. Amen.

And without faith it is impossible to please God, because anyone who comes to him must believe that he exists and that he rewards those who earnestly seek him.

—Hebrews 11:6

Nine

SEEK

Seek [seek]
—verb *(used with object)* To go in search or quest of: *to seek the truth*. To try to find or discover by searching or questioning: *to seek the solution to a problem*. To try to obtain: *to seek fame*.

My prayer journal for January 1, 2002, reads: "As this baby year ticks away its first day, my prayer, my goal, is to seek the Lord my God in all my dealings. In all I am and long to be. This is my word for 2002—*seek*."

If any word could be the centerpiece of my life, it would be *seek*. From the moment I first made the decision to follow Jesus, I actively sought Him. I made a promise to God that I would read the Bible every day. I've kept that promise for forty years now. I don't say this to pat myself on the back because had it become a chore, I don't think I could have fulfilled that promise. All I had to do was seek God—open my Bible. The word *seek* is an action word. When I took that first step, out of obedience and because of my promise, God spoke to me. As I read His Word, I hear His voice loud and clear. It's the one time in my day that I can be still and get direction. It orders my whole schedule and I wouldn't miss it for the world.

When we seek Him, the rewards are so rich that we soon realize we can't afford to stop. It's like getting a chance to have breakfast with your favorite friend—the one you just can't seem to get enough of. Would you consider this opportunity a drudge?

In *The Christian Light of Life*, Reverend Dr. Valson Thampu gives some guidelines for seeking God. In part, he says we need to:

> Seek him daily (Isaiah 58:2). Jesus taught us to pray, "Give us this day our daily bread."
>
> Seek Him early (Proverbs 1:28; Psalm 63:1). Seeking God must be a passion and a priority, not a mechanical obligation.
>
> Seek diligently (Proverbs 7:15).
>
> Seek His face continuously (1 Chronicles 16:11).
>
> Seek God with all your heart (Deuteronomy 4:29).[1]

Seeking must be intentional. My normal routine is to rise at 3:55 A.M. to start my day with prayer and Bible study. Diligently, continuously, with all our hearts—these are the keys to seeking God.

I discovered a moving story of one young woman's passionate seeking for God. Mary Jones woke each morning in her *croglofft* bed to the sound of a soft wind blowing over the Cader Idris Mountain in her native North Wales. Though her father was a weaver, their family was poor, even by village standards. They lived in a cottage of rubble walls with a single window and a door on the front and a thick gable end incorporating a hearth and chimney. The *croglofft*, or loft, reached by a ladder, gave some additional sleeping space under the thatched roof. The Joneses may not have had an extra copper halfpenny to spare, but Mary was better off than many girls in the last decade of the eighteenth century, because Mary could read. The Reverend Thomas Charles, a preacher from the town of Bala, used to come to Mary's town of Gwynedd when he could to give lessons. He believed girls should read as well as boys, so Mary never missed a class.

When Reverend Charles took out his worn Bible and handed it to Mary to read aloud to the class she handled it carefully. The leather binding was worn but it felt warm to her touch. Maybe because Reverend Charles always kept it tucked in his vest, next to his shirt. She couldn't imagine what it would be like to have a Bible all to oneself.

When Reverend Charles was not in town she would walk the two miles to a neighboring farm to read their Bible. But more than anything else, Mary longed to have a Bible of her own. She began to figure out how she could save money to buy a Bible. She began helping in the mill when there was extra carding to be done, taking in laundry, and doing chores for neighbors.

The only place to buy a Bible was from Reverend Charles in his village, Bala, twenty-five miles away. It took Mary six years to save enough up enough money to purchase a Bible. When she finally added the last coin to the stack she tied them up in a *cadach* and tucked the cloth deep in her apron pocket. Reverend Charles had been visiting so infrequently of late she didn't want to wait for him to come to Gwynedd. She'd then have to wait until his next trip to have her Bible. She was fifteen years old. She'd walk to Bala.

One morning in 1800, her mother packed some food in a satchel and Mary set off. She had no shoes but she was used to walking barefoot. Besides, she would have to ford streams, walk up mountain trails, and take paths through the valleys. It would be much easier without the encumbrance of shoes. As she walked, her hand kept feeling the bundle of coins. She had never thought this day would come.

When she finally arrived at Reverend Charles's home she found all the Bibles he had had already been sold or spoken for. Mary couldn't hold her tears back. She picked up one of the reserved Bibles and asked if she could read it for a little while. Reverend Charles was so moved by the girl's hunger for the Word he let her buy the reserved Bible, deciding the other purchaser could wait a bit more.

Mary's desire for the Bible profoundly impacted Thomas Charles. He knew other seekers longed for a Bible just as fervently as Mary had. He proposed to the council of the Religious Tract Society to form a new society to supply Wales with Bibles. And, in 1804, the British and Foreign Bible Society was established in London.

Mary Jones died in 1864 and was buried at the graveyard of Bryn-crug Calvinistic Methodist Chapel. Her Bible is now housed in the Bible Society's archives in Cambridge University Library.[2]

Mary Jones was a seeker. She longed for things of the Lord. That's what I always want.

Who's Seeking Whom?

My friend chose the same word for her 2011 word—*seek*. She shared her journal entry with me:

> While I was at the retreat, one of the women told how her alarm clock was set for 6:33 A.M. every morning. What a strange time. I asked about it and she said it was in honor of Matthew 6:33: "Seek ye first the kingdom of God and His righteousness . . ."
>
> Since "seek" is my word for this year I decided to adopt the 6:33 wake-up call so I can spend a good hour seeking the Lord before anyone else stirs. I set the clock radio alarm without realizing it was tuned to an oldies station. It came on at exactly 6:33 with the very first notes of the song, "I Will Follow Him." It totally cracked me up. Subtle? Not. Who is seeking whom?
>
> When I opened my prayer journal the verse I had to meditate on was Psalm 63:1: "O God, you are my God, earnestly I seek you; my soul thirsts for you, in a dry and weary land where there is no water." Earnestly I seek you.
>
> Not likely to be coincidence. My Bible Study today focused on the Exodus where God said He would satisfy the thirsty and fill the hungry. I love how He designs our interaction. All I need do is seek Him.

Tragedy as Motivation

What causes us to seek God? Sometimes this appetite grows out of tragic circumstances. We don't often hear about the childhoods of historic figures, but William Bradford, the Pilgrim governor of the fledging Plymouth Colony, had the kind of childhood that would emotionally cripple many men. He was born in Austerfield, England, but before he was out of leading strings, at only sixteen months of age, his father died. He was too young to have known the man he was named after, but the death must have left a gaping hole in his life. His mother remarried when he was only four but instead of getting a new father, for some reason, he was sent to live with his grandfather. Sadly, this was not to be the security it should have been for the young William. His grandfather died just two years later and William, who'd already suffered more than his share of loss, went back to live with his mother and stepfather. A year later his mother died and the seven-year-old was shuttled off to the home of his two uncles, who were happy enough to have another potential worker for their farm.

That didn't work out because William became chronically ill and was not able to do manual labor. His uncles allowed him instead to take lessons with a local minister—a very unusual opportunity for a commoner in the 1600s. William devoured the Bible and whatever books he was able to read. He was hungry to know God and to know more about Him. When he was twelve, still frail and weak but no longer sick, William happened upon an unusual church service in the nearby town of Scrooby. It was nothing like the Church of England services he was accustomed to. William was struck by the lack of ritual and the genuine sense of fellowship. In his journal he later wrote of these Separatists, as they were called, "[They] laboured to have ye right worship of God & discipline of Christ established in ye church, according to ye simplicitie of ye gospell, without the mixture of mens inventions, and to have & to be ruled by ye laws of Gods word."

It was at this church that he met William Brewster, who became like a father and mentor to him. When these Pilgrims discovered that King James I intended to "harry them from the land," they set sail for the Netherlands, where they settled for a dozen years until unrest there sent them on their way to the New World aboard a tiny ship, the *Mayflower.*

William Bradford's journal *Of Plimoth Plantation* is the single most complete story of the birth of our nation—all from an unlikely orphan who, but for God's intervention, should have grown up to be an English farmer. William Bradford, the seeker, served as governor of Plymouth Colony for more than thirty years.[3]

REWARDS FOR SEEKING GOD

Seeking God changes us. It frees us to live deeper, richer lives. The Bible is full of promises for those who seek God. Dr. Thampu lists some of these:

> God gives understanding to those who seek Him (Psalm 53:2).
> Those who seek the Lord abide in Him (Psalm 119:45).
> To seek the Lord is to live in a state of contentment (Psalm 23:1 and 34:10).
> Those who seek the Lord are free from petty worries about what they will eat, drink, or wear (Matthew 6:25).
> They will not be lonely or forsaken (Psalm 9:10).
> Those who seek the Lord are joyful (Psalm 70:4 and 105:3).
> Those who seek the Lord live life in all its fullness (Amos 5:4).[4]

I often see the bumper sticker at Christmastime: WISE MEN STILL SEEK HIM. I explored the word *seek* in depth for one year in 2002, but it has become part of my life.

CHOOSING YOUR WORD

When you've chosen your own word, be sure to record any promises that come with your word. For instance, let's say your word is *restoration*. Jeremiah 30:17 says, " 'I will restore you to health and heal your wounds,' declares the LORD." That's some promise, isn't it? How about 1 Peter 5:10: "And the God of all grace, who called you to his eternal glory in Christ, after you have suffered a little while, will himself restore you and make you strong, firm and steadfast." Make a collection of the promises. God keeps His word, so those promises are for you.

WORDPLAY

Consider creating a scrapbook of your words and some of the things you've learned about each. If you are not familiar with the craft, classes are readily available in the art of scrapbooking. Supplies are generally inexpensive and it's a great way to literally get your hands around your word.

From My Prayer Journal

Father God, open my mind and my heart to You. Like a child sitting in rapt attention—that's the way I want to be when it comes to hearing Your wonderful voice. I long to see each day unfold with lessons from You. Lessons about love and wisdom, harmony and joy. I want to be a child. Your child. Amen.

There is a time for everything,
and a season for every activity under the heavens:
a time to be born and a time to die,
a time to plant and a time to uproot,
a time to kill and a time to heal,
a time to tear down and a time to build,
a time to weep and a time to laugh,
a time to mourn and a time to dance,
a time to scatter stones and a time to gather them,
a time to embrace and a time to refrain from embracing,
a time to search and a time to give up,
a time to keep and a time to throw away,
a time to tear and a time to mend,
a time to be silent and a time to speak,
a time to love and a time to hate,
a time for war and a time for peace.
—Ecclesiastes 3:1–8

Ten

BALANCE

Bal·ance [bal-*uh*ns]
—noun A state of equilibrium or equipoise; equal distribution of weight, amount, etc. Something used to produce equilibrium; counterpoise. Mental steadiness or emotional stability; habit of calm behavior, judgment, etc.

In 2009, I chose the word *balance*. I'm sure I don't have to explain why. Hardly a day goes by when we don't hear someone say they are seeking balance in their life. I've been working on it for a very long time. I have a number of strategies for this, but it is an ongoing battle. There are simply too many opportunities, too many people, too much work, too many play temptations, too many needs up against too little time and sometimes, too few resources.

It's no wonder we are stressed.

Finding balance in my life has been a struggle for as long as I can remember—but it's getting a little better every year. I'm making progress, although at times it feels just the opposite. The

challenge is to balance our spiritual life, family, friends, relationships, work, health, and personal interests in one integrated
pattern.

DETERMINE YOUR PRIORITIES

It's important to lay the groundwork for a balanced life. In order
to put first things first, we need to determine our priorities and
put them in order. For me, it's God first, then family, then work.
The others—friends, relationships, health, and personal interests (read: knitting, traveling, reading, cooking)—slide around
depending on the season and the circumstances. But all of these
things are vitally important to me.

Each one of us will be different. Some people struggle, for
instance, to make work a priority. With me, I love my work and
I have to work to keep it from taking over.

Be brutally honest when you set your priorities. Look at
the time you currently expend on activities. This will give you
an unbiased indication of where your true priorities lie. If you
believe God is your number one priority, but the only time
you spend with Him is an hour or two Sunday morning, it's time
to reassess. If you spend three hours a day on Facebook, e-mail,
and online solitaire, you need to examine that against the hour
you spend talking to your family.

Charles Grandison Finney was one of the most successful
American revival preachers in history—and a man who sought
balance and well-ordered priorities. He is directly credited with
the conversion of nearly half a million people. He was a folk
hero to the masses and packed out venues everywhere he went.
George Williams decided to follow Christ after reading Finney's

writings. He was so inspired by Finney's stand on social reform, Williams started the YMCA.

Finney spent many years as a professor at Oberlin College. The college was controversial from the day it opened its doors because it not only admitted people of color but allowed women to study alongside men. Oberlin was a very active stop on the Underground Railroad, inflaming sentiment against the "radical" institution. Many of the people involved were ardent abolitionists, including Finney and the very wealthy Tappen brothers, who poured money into the institution and the causes they espoused.

Finney believed slaveholding was a sin and irreconcilable with Christianity in the day in which he lived. But despite his firmly held beliefs and outspokenness on the subject throughout his entire career, he was criticized by the Tappens for not taking a strong enough stand on abolition.

What the Tappens didn't understand was that Charles Finney sought balance in his life and ministry. He knew he was called to be an evangelist first. He believed that when people turned over their lives to Christ there would be social transformation, not just reform. Finney had a firm grip on his calling and he understood his priorities. The work he did in spiritual transformation is legendary, but the outgrowth of that was changed lives through social transformation as well.[1]

SET GOALS

Setting goals is a key element of living a balanced life. One of my own affirmations is "My life is focused and filled with purpose." In the years when my children were young we worked on goals together on New Year's Day. I've continued the same rhythm—assessing and setting goals in time for the new year.

Remember to always set SMART goals:

- **S—Specific.** Rather than say you want to spend more time with your grown daughter, why not say you plan to do one activity—go to lunch, go shopping, bake together—each month?

- **M—Measurable.** In the previous example you should be able to measure your results at the end of the year. "We spent eleven out of the optimal twelve days together."

- **A—Attainable.** When setting goals, it's easy to get carried away with optimism. Make sure they are realistic or you will doom yourself to failure before you even begin.

- **R—Rewarding.** Make sure the goals you set are in line with your priorities. There has to be an innate reward in accomplishing the goals. For instance, I love to knit. If I set a goal to finish one project for each grandchild in the year, I'm meeting two priorities—family and personal interests—and I'm blocking out specific time to do something I find rewarding.

- **T—Time-bound.** When you set a deadline you ensure that the goal will move forward. Using my knitting example, if I turned the calendar page to November and still had two knitting projects to complete, I'd make sure to devote more time in the evening to knitting. Or I might take my knitting with me to meetings and appointments.

DREAM

If you want to live a balanced life, don't overlook the importance of dreaming. I believe we need to give ourselves permission to carve out space to dream. I have a friend who works in the art field. In order to come up with new designs she sets aside a day or days to wallow in ideas, colors, stories, and textures. As she says, you can't create out of an empty reservoir.

In the same way, we need to schedule time to dream and, if our surroundings are too distracting, perhaps find an out-of-the-way place to do so. When you reach the end of your life, what things would you like to have accomplished? If you could do one thing for yourself, what would it be? Forgetting circumstances, how would you finish this statement: "I wish . . . ?"

It's like working a muscle: unless you exercise your capacity to dream, your thinking is hindered and grows weak. Don't be afraid to stretch beyond your comfort zone. Dream often and dream big.

Once you've spent time dreaming, look hard at those dreams. Is there any reason you can't turn them into long-term goals? What would it take? Every time you come up with a roadblock, try to pair it with a solution.

And it doesn't matter how old you are. Lottie Moon, the beloved missionary, once said, "I have a firm conviction that I am immortal till my work is done."

PRAY

If you long for balance, lay your dreams, priorities, and goals before the Lord and pray over them. Repeatedly. Be open to revision if you hear that still, small voice. This is what Richard Chichester, a thirteenth-century English saint, prayed:

> *May I know Thee more clearly*
> *Love Thee more dearly*
> *Follow Thee more nearly.*[2]

ARISE, SHINE

You might be one of those people who claim not to be a morning person. I have a friend who used to insist that all early risers had to constantly repent from a touch of smugness. This same friend is now rising at five thirty A.M. to tackle all the things she wants to have in her life. I know it may not be right for everyone, but when you rise early and start your day with quiet time, exercise, Bible study, and prayer, you will open up a whole new dimension in your life. There's just something about seeing the sun rise every morning while sipping a hot cup of tea or coffee in a silent house. There's a hush that is almost holy.

ORGANIZE

I am not an organizational expert, but if you want to have enough time to stay in balance, you need systems to give you the time to accomplish all you want to accomplish. I have a friend who thrives on organization. Nothing makes her happier than finding a new system to organize a closet, outfit a handbag, or store DVDs. She never has to waste time looking for anything. Her filing systems are intuitive. Anyone could walk into her house and slip into her system without skipping a beat. It takes time to set up, but there are rich dividends. If this is not your gift, there are a number of books and websites that teach organization, or if you are willing to invest in getting organized, there are organizers to coach you.

Organization extends beyond environmental organization. You will save time if your household chores, like grocery shopping and children's lessons and sports events, are organized. Keeping calendars, having greeting cards on hand (stored in appropriate files), logging schedules of car maintenance—all these things will simplify your life.

It's important to remember that the opposite of organization is chaos. And chaos causes upheavals that gobble up time and energy.

De-clutter

De-cluttering goes hand in hand with organization. Clutter is distracting and wastes time. If you have a stack of something on a counter, it's a sign that a new system is needed to address that clutter. For example, rather than keep upcoming invitations in a stack by the phone, process them when they come in. Decide whether or not you'll attend and RSVP. Put the date on the calendar with pertinent information. If you'll need a gift, take out the shopping list and add it. File the invitation in a file folder marked "Upcoming Events," clipping the map to the invitation.

Now, instead of leaving the RSVP until late enough to exasperate the host, you've responded early. Instead of forgetting the gift until the very morning of the event and having to fit it in between soccer practice, returning books to the library, and grocery shopping, you have it waiting in the gift area of a closet. Instead of forgetting details about the event and having to call a friend, it's all on your calendar. And if you need more details, you can put your hand on the invitation in less than a minute. Then once you're ready to go out the door you don't have to look around for directions—it's all in one place. All because you wanted to de-clutter one harmless little stack.

Create Allies

If you live in a family, you need to enlist everyone as an ally. Wayne and I talk about and share goals so we can help one another. If you are married, it is especially important for a couple to help one another successfully attain balance. If your wife knows it is one of your goals to play golf once each month, she's going to help you set aside that time. If your husband knows you long to be a published author, he's going to sacrifice so you have the time you need. Or rent you a typewriter, as my husband did for me in those days before home computers.

Review

Periodically take out your goals and do a checkup. How are you coming along? What do you need to step up? What needs to come back into balance?

At the end of the year it's time to do a serious debrief. How'd you do overall? What exceeded your expectations? What didn't work? What could you have changed to make it work? Are there any goals that don't matter anymore? Are there more you need to consider?

Don't get discouraged if you didn't accomplish every goal. If you did, you may have aimed too low. Last year I wrote down sixty-eight achievable goals and managed to see almost 80 percent of them come to fruition. At the start of each week I reviewed my goals, which are divided into a number of specific areas to chart my progress. This way I keep them fresh in my mind. I believe that just reading over them helps my subconscious mind start working on helping me to achieve these goals.

Remember, no matter how impossible things may seem, we, by the grace of God, are in control of how we choose to view them. I think of Anne Frank seeking balance in a world gone crazy. Here's what she said in her diary on Tuesday, March 7, 1944: "I've found that there is always some beauty left—in nature, sunshine, freedom, in yourself; these can all help you. Look at these things, then find yourself again, and God, and then regain your balance . . . He who has courage and faith will never perish in misery!"[3]

CHOOSING YOUR WORD

When you have your word chosen for the year, you might want to develop a reading plan to go with it. It's a great way to dig deeper into your word. How do you find the key books about your subject? One of your best resources would be a Christian bookstore. Ask the bookseller to name the classic books on your subject. Then ask for any new, important books. You can also research online. If you go to Christianbooks.com, for instance, you can quickly get a feel for the key books and read reviews as well. If your church has a library, the librarian might be able to help, or maybe even your pastor. Reading the wisdom of others will only deepen your exploration of your word.

WORDPLAY

You may already know that I'm an avid knitter. I could get excited about knitting a new prayer shawl with my word bordering the edges done in an embroidery technique. What fun to be literally cloaked in the Word and in my chosen word of the year.

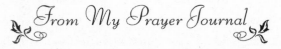

From My Prayer Journal

Lord, I long to serve You all the days of my life. From the moment I crawl out of bed in the morning until I turn off the last light each night. When I am buried may those who come to celebrate my life declare how much I loved the Lord. Amen.

If any of you lacks wisdom, you should ask
God, who gives generously to all without
finding fault, and it will be given to you.

—James 1:5

Eleven

WISDOM

Wis·dom [*wiz*-duhm]
—noun The quality or state of being wise; knowledge of what is true or right coupled with just judgment as to action; sagacity, discernment, or insight. Scholarly knowledge or learning. Sayings or teachings; precepts.

The year was 2005 and the word I chose was *wisdom*. Here's what I wrote in my journal:

Generally, on the first day of the year, I write a few picturesque lines about the upcoming year. The year 2004 was a year of tremendous joy and horrific pain. And as 2005 is here, I am left to wonder what the days and weeks will hold for me and those I love.

I already have the word for the year. As it always happens, God presented it to me early in the day, wisdom. *I've been praying for godly wisdom and to seek more of*

Him and His Word in my life. God's Word promises to supply abundantly to all who seek His wisdom.

This is a good start for the year for me, a sign that reminds me all is in His almighty hands. Wayne and I spent New Year's in the Florida Panhandle and came home around 4:00. After unpacking the car, I collected all my devotional books together, unwilling to start the New Year without spending time with God.

SEEKING WISDOM

It's easy to say we want to seek wisdom, but how does one go about doing it? In Andy Andrews's book *The Traveler's Gift*, he proposes an effective action plan:

Knowing that wisdom waits to be gathered, I actively search her out. I will change my actions TODAY! I will train my eyes and ears to read and listen to books and recordings that bring about positive changes in my personal relationships and a greater understanding of my fellow man. I will read and listen only to what increases my belief in myself and my future.

I will seek wisdom. I will choose my friends with care.

I am who my friends are. I speak their language, and I wear their clothes. I share their opinions and their habits. From this moment forward, I will choose to associate with people whose lives and lifestyles I admire. If I associate with chickens, I will learn to scratch at the ground and squabble over crumbs. If I associate with eagles,

I will learn to soar to great heights. I am an eagle. It is my destiny to fly.

I will seek wisdom. I will listen to the counsel of wise men.

The words of a wise man are like raindrops on dry ground. They are precious and can be quickly used for immediate results. Only the blade of grass that catches a raindrop will prosper and grow.

I will seek wisdom. I will be a servant to others.

A wise man will cultivate a servant's spirit, for that particular attribute attracts people like no other. As I humbly serve others, their wisdom will be freely shared with me. He who serves the most grows the fastest.

I will become a humble servant. I will look to open the door for someone. I will be excited when I am available to help. I will be a servant to others. I will listen to the counsel of wise men. I will choose my friends with care.

I will seek wisdom.[1]

I know that Andy Andrews knows the Source of all wisdom, but I would add to his list to seek the God of wisdom. When we seek God, wisdom is a result.

THE WISDOM OF SOLOMON

Another great action plan for seeking wisdom is to spend time in the book of Proverbs. The Lord says in Proverbs 2:2, if you are "turning your ear to wisdom and applying your heart to understanding—" you will ultimately understand and find knowledge. Proverbs consists of thirty-one chapters, each one jam-packed with wisdom. Penned by Solomon and other writers, and inspired by the Holy Spirit, the wisdom in Proverbs is as relevant today as it was over three thousand years ago.

King Solomon wasn't born extraordinarily wise. He asked God for the gift of wisdom. One night early in Solomon's reign, the Lord appeared to him in a dream and said, "Ask for whatever you want me to give you."

Can you imagine being given that opportunity? What would you ask for? Riches? Health? Happiness? Not Solomon. He answered,

> You have shown great kindness to your servant, my father David, because he was faithful to you and righteous and upright in heart. You have continued this great kindness to him and have given him a son to sit on his throne this very day.
>
> Now, Lord my God, you have made your servant king in place of my father David. But I am only a little child and do not know how to carry out my duties. Your servant is here among the people you have chosen, a great people, too numerous to count or number. So give your servant a discerning heart to govern your people and to distinguish between right and wrong. For who is able to govern this great people of yours? (1 Kings 3:6–9)

The Bible says the Lord was pleased with his request. God answered that prayer and wisdom became the hallmark of Solomon's reign. Once, two women were brought before him. Here's the account of that story from the Bible:

> One of them said, "Pardon me, my lord. This woman and I live in the same house, and I had a baby while she was

there with me. The third day after my child was born, this woman also had a baby. We were alone; there was no one in the house but the two of us.

"During the night this woman's son died because she lay on him. So she got up in the middle of the night and took my son from my side while I your servant was asleep. She put him by her breast and put her dead son by my breast. The next morning, I got up to nurse my son—and he was dead! But when I looked at him closely in the morning light, I saw that it wasn't the son I had borne."

The other woman said, "No! The living one is my son; the dead one is yours."

But the first one insisted, "No! The dead one is yours; the living one is mine." And so they argued before the king.

The king said, "This one says, 'My son is alive and your son is dead,' while that one says, 'No! Your son is dead and mine is alive.'"

Then the king said, "Bring me a sword." So they brought a sword for the king. He then gave an order: "Cut the living child in two and give half to one and half to the other."

The woman whose son was alive was deeply moved out of love for her son and said to the king, "Please, my lord, give her the living baby! Don't kill him!"

But the other said, "Neither I nor you shall have him. Cut him in two!"

Then the king gave his ruling: "Give the living baby to the first woman. Do not kill him; she is his mother."

When all Israel heard the verdict the king had given, they held the king in awe, because they saw that he

had wisdom from God to administer justice. (1 Kings
3:17–28)

Solomon's wisdom allowed him to look past the surface to find
the truth.

WISDOM LOOKS PAST THE SURFACE

In 1976, Elizabeth Silance Ballard wrote a short story for
HomeLife magazine. It's been copied over and over, often by
people claiming the story is their own true story, but in her short
piece of fiction Miss Ballard illustrated the wisdom of looking
deeper.

She tells of meeting ten-year-old Teddy Stallard for the first
time in her fifth-grade classroom many years before. She took an
immediate dislike to the boy. This troubled her because teachers
try very hard not to have favorites and even harder not to harbor
negative feelings about any students but, she was ashamed to
admit, Teddy made her skin crawl. His unkempt, overlong hair
would fall into his eyes as he tried to write. And the smell! It
made it hard to be near to him for any length of time.

Within the first week she knew she needed to be close to
him, smell or not, because he was hopelessly behind the other
students. He read haltingly and seemed to take forever to catch
on to things. Slow. The boy was just plain slow. The teacher
couldn't help herself. She withdrew from the boy every time he
came near.

She knew that a good teacher spent time and effort with the
slower children, knowing that the bright students would keep
up no matter what. She was ashamed to admit it, but that year

she lavished time on the more promising students and avoided Teddy. She even took a perverse pleasure in marking up his papers—red all over them. Almost as if to prove she was right about him. She never ridiculed Teddy, but kids read attitude far better than words, and her students knew how she felt about the boy.

Teddy seemed to sense how she felt as well.

As the year passed, the teacher couldn't seem to stem her intense dislike for her student. When the time came for Christmas break it was apparent that Teddy would never make it to the next grade. He'd be spending a second year in fifth grade.

To justify herself the teacher checked the school records on Teddy. The first-grade teacher had commented that Teddy showed great promise but had a "poor home situation." The second year someone noted that his mother was terminally ill and that he had little support at home. In third grade the teacher wrote that he was a pleasant boy but struggling. Another note at the end of that year simply stated, "Mother passed away." His fourth-grade teacher wrote that Teddy was very well behaved but slow. She added that the father showed no interest.

The teacher closed the file and felt justified. He was a good candidate for retention. He'd be repeating fifth grade.

On the day before Christmas vacation the classroom buzzed with excited children. Each child had brought a gift for the teacher and tucked it under the little classroom Christmas tree. As she opened the gifts, the teacher exclaimed over each one. Teddy's gift came about halfway through the pile. It was clumsily wrapped in a brown paper bag.

The children watched the teacher's every move as she started to unwrap the thing. Before she could even manage to get the paper bag unwound two items fell out of the wrapping—a cheap rhinestone bracelet with many of the stones missing and a dime store bottle of perfume, only half full. The students began to whisper and then the giggles and snickers started.

The teacher stopped and looked at Teddy's face. She couldn't miss the intensity. She took the bracelet and draped it over her wrist. She then asked Teddy to help her fasten it. The boy came hesitantly forward and fumbled with the clasp until he had it fastened. The children looked uncertain as she lifted her arm and let the bracelet sparkle as it caught the light. She then dabbed the cologne behind her ear and let the girls line up to get a little dab behind theirs. She continued to open the gifts until it was time for refreshments and the closing bell. The children filed out of the room, shouting "Merry Christmas!" as they ran to start their holidays.

All except Teddy.

"You smell just like my mom," he said shyly as he moved toward her desk. He touched the bracelet and told her that it had also been his mom's. After he left, the teacher went to her desk surrounded by all the beautiful gifts the children had brought. She cleared a space, put her head down, and wept, fingering the gaudy bracelet. What kind of teacher was she? She decided right then and there to be the kind of teacher Teddy needed. No, she wanted to be the kind of teacher all the children needed.

From January 2 to the end of school she stayed with Teddy every afternoon. Sometimes they worked together and other times she graded papers while he worked alone. Little by little he began to catch up to the rest of the class. By the end of the year his grades were near the top of the class.

Needless to say, he did not have to repeat fifth grade.

The teacher lost track of Teddy until a letter came one day. Teddy wrote that he was graduating high school second in his class. "I wanted you to be the first to know," he wrote. She sent him a pen and pencil set to commemorate the event. She wondered what he would do after graduation.

Four years later she received another letter. Teddy would be graduating first in his class from college. First! He wrote that it had been tough, but he would surely miss it. His once reticent teacher was so proud. She bought him a pair of sterling monogrammed cuff links. Who would've thought . . . ?

But the day she would never forget was the day she received his third letter. He wrote that he was now Theodore J. Stallard, MD, and not only that, but he was getting married. He said that he had no family since his father died the year before. This one-time outcast, this once lost little boy wrote to ask his fifth-grade teacher if she would come to the wedding and sit in the place where his mom would have sat.

I can imagine the fragrance and jewelry she wore to that wedding.[2]

Bits of Homespun Wisdom

When I choose a word, it always makes me more sensitive to seeing it in practice, even when it's demonstrated by my grand-kids. Just this year, Cameron, who recently turned thirteen, had me laughing so hard I could barely breathe. His sister, her parents' only girl, with two brothers, has learned to hold her own. She got into a squabble with her brother, and her parents put her in time-out. Cameron came to me and with all the wisdom of his years announced, "Maddy's got issues, but if you mention it, she beats you up." It's a wise brother who knows to steer clear of a girl with issues.

I'd like to think wisdom runs in our family. My precious one-hundred-year-old aunt Betty Stierwalt wrote me before I went in for knee replacement surgery. Actually, her *sore left leg* wrote my *damaged right knee* a letter filled with encouragement and advice. She insists that she's going to live until she dies. That, my friends, is profound advice.

REWARDS FOR SEEKING WISDOM

As I've discovered with so many of our words, when we seek wisdom we end up receiving far more than expected. Here are some of the rewards for seeking wisdom:

- You'll be rewarded with good understanding (Psalm 111:10).
- You'll be rewarded with wisdom (James 1:5).
- You'll be rewarded with a future hope that won't be cut off (Proverbs 24:14).
- You'll be rewarded by having your life preserved (Ecclesiastes 7:11–12).
- You'll be rewarded with power (Ecclesiastes 7:19).

WISDOM IS NO RESPECTER OF AGE

Not long after I chose the word that year, I was watching the news and recorded this in my journal:

> *There was a young football player penalized fifteen yards because after he scored a touchdown, he got down on*

one knee and praised God by looking up to Heaven and raising his open palm to God—just saying thank You.

The reporters kept trying to get him to say something against the referee or the whole system for penalizing him for praying.

When they questioned him, he answered, "Well, the rules say that there would be no end zone arrogance."

Of course, the interviewers said, "Well, you weren't arrogant. You were just praising God."

"But that's what the rules say," he quietly answered.

So the reporter tried a different approach. "Well, if you do that, if you score again, will you do the same thing?"

"That's something I need to talk over with my coach."

I was overwhelmed by the wisdom of this junior high athlete who refused to offer a negative slant though given every opportunity. Wisdom has nothing to do with age. In a case like this, it is so obvious it comes from God.

A Legacy of Wisdom

A friend wrote an article about the importance of leaving a legacy of wisdom behind for our children. She received a letter from a reader that she shared with me. The Reverend James McWhorter wrote in part:

It has been my desire for a long time to pass on something to my succeeding generations. Several years ago I typed a letter to be given to each of my grandchildren on their thirteenth birthday. I have already given this to two biological grandchildren and one step-granddaughter. Upon [the grandchild's] turning thirteen I take the grandchild to a special event on which we have agreed. (Fishing trip, Pro Basketball game, an evening at Medieval Times.) While en route to the special event I give them a speech concerning their responsibility as a young adult. My dad had a similar talk with me at about the same age and it stuck with me all my life. I tell them some things my father told me about work ethics, responsibility and I add some things about Christian responsibility. I then give them my seven-page letter which contains a personalized note to that particular grandchild and my own testimony. This letter is placed in a pocket folder notebook and is to be passed down with a similar letter from each generation to the next. I jokingly call it our Baptist, Gentile bar mitzvah.

I can picture a thirteen-year-old grandchild rolling his eyes at Grandpa's speech, but you know that child will remember that day forever. That's passing wisdom from one generation to the next.

Proverbs 4:7 says, "Wisdom is supreme; therefore get wisdom. Though it cost all you have, get understanding." That's wise advice: *get wisdom.*

CHOOSING YOUR WORD

You've heard me say that I wait for my word each year until I sense God in the choice. One of the most absorbing questions is how we recognize the "voice" of God. For centuries—

millennia, really—Christians have obsessed over the challenge of how to discern God's voice. I'd never be so bold as to categorically state, "God said . . ." Yes, it can happen that way. It certainly did in the Bible, but in my experience God usually speaks in a still, small voice. He speaks through His Word and through His people. And we have to listen very intently to all of those to discern His voice.

So when I say listen to God for your word, I'm saying take time to think about it, pray about it, be aware as you read your Bible, and wait. You'll start to get a sense. A hint. Then you'll hear it from a different source. You may open a book and there's the word again. You sit down to have lunch with a friend and the word comes up in conversation. Be patient. You'll know.

WORDPLAY

Years ago, a quilt exhibit toured the country. My friend saw it in Oakland, California. The quilts were exquisite—examples of every kind, from album quilts to crazy quilts—but the one collection my friend has never forgotten was a display of quilts all created by one turn-of-the-last-century quilter. The woman had spent her entire life creating what must have been colorful quilts in rich detail with tiny, near-perfect stitching and imaginative patterns. But she hit a rough patch in her life and fell into a deep depression. One morning she woke and decided to dye all her quilts black. Her life's work. It must have taken her all day and more and a huge tub of dye, but all the quilts were shades of black. The quilts were still beautiful because each patch absorbed the dye differently, giving a subtle shading that was artful and sophisticated. But even more compelling was the story behind the quilts.

That's what a quilt or collection of quilts becomes—a story. I can just imagine what a treasure a quilt combining all my life words would be. Or can you picture one quilt every year centered around that year's word? The life work of that quilter would be both a treasured collection and a testimony in textile.

From My Prayer Journal

Dear Lord, this day is traditionally known as April Fool's Day, but it is this day that I read 1 Kings 3:9 in which Solomon asks You for abundant wisdom to govern his people. If I'm a fool, then I want to be a fool for You. As for my request, I, too, would ask You for the wisdom to be the woman You long for me to be, and the insight and knowledge to write books that turn people toward You. Amen.

Trust in the L<small>ORD</small> *with all your heart and lean not on your own understanding; in all your ways submit to him, and he will make your paths straight.*
—Proverbs 3:5–6

Twelve

SURRENDER

Sur·ren·der [suh-*ren*-der]
—verb *(used with object)* To yield (something) to the possession or power of another; deliver up possession of on demand
or under duress. To give (oneself) up, as to the police. To give
(oneself) up to some influence, course, emotion, etc.: *He surrendered himself to a life of hardship.*

The year was 2004 and my word for the year was *surrender*.
It's interesting to read the opening pages of my journal and
see how the word surprised me. I began as I so often did—
philosophical about a blank slate and a new year. And then the
word hit me and I froze. Here's what I wrote:

> *I love it when I start a new journal. I come at it with
> fresh enthusiasm and such optimism for the future, con-
> fident in the love of my heavenly Father and His care for
> me and for those I cherish.*
>
> *A journal is like a snowy landscape just waiting for*

footprints to mark the scene. I'm ready to take this jour-
ney onward across freshly fallen snow, pristine in beauty,
clear and confident of my course. I can because of Christ
and the role He plays in every aspect of my life.

I spent the Christmas holidays with my parents. My
father is failing and my mother is becoming more and
more confused. We learned late yesterday afternoon that
Dad is in the hospital. He'll need to go into some kind of
assisted living very soon.

As I was going through my e-mails, it came to me that
my word for the year was surrender. A sense of forebod-
ing and fear came over me. I'd like to think of myself as
a woman of faith, and I was ashamed that I should have
such lack of trust in God. I don't even know exactly what
it is that I fear. It's just so hard to think of the future
without my dad.

My dad did indeed die that year, on February 21, and
I learned whole new lessons about surrender, especially when
we have to surrender those we love to the arms of Jesus.

But surrender is mostly about letting go and being willing to
stand with empty arms and an empty heart until God fills and
renews us once more.

GETTING OVER OURSELVES

Too many times we shy away from surrender because it seems
passive, as if we're resigned. The words that come to mind are
troubling: to give up, to blindly accept the status quo. We think
of laziness, failure to act, inability to take things in our own
hands. All negative to our way of thinking.

Why is surrender so counterintuitive? Maybe it's because it is such a complex concept. And it's the key to a real spiritual breakthrough. It's getting to the very end of ourselves. Maybe even getting over ourselves.

C. S. Lewis, in his book *Mere Christianity*, says, "The more we let Him take us over, the more truly ourselves we become. He invented—as an author invents characters in a novel—all the different [people] that you and I were intended to be . . . It is when I turn to Christ, when I give myself up to His Personality, that I first begin to have a real personality of my own."[1]

In other words, we have to lose ourselves to find ourselves.

COUNTING THE COST

History offers many examples of people who sacrificed for others. Irena Sendler grew up in Poland and, wanting to help people, studied at Warsaw University to become a social worker. Who would have guessed that because of the times she lived in, she'd be required to surrender everything to accomplish that?

Irena was a Christian, so when Hitler began his rise to power, she was under no immediate threat. Had she just kept her head down and gone about her life, she could have made it through those troubled times with little risk. But that was not to be.

"I was taught that if you see a person drowning," she said, "you must jump into the water to save them, whether you can swim or not." At thirty years old and not even topping five feet, that's exactly what she did.

In 1940, when the Nazis began rounding up the Jews in Poland and herding them into the Warsaw Ghetto, Irena couldn't stop thinking about what kind of misery must be going on behind the high walls they'd built around the area. Social workers were not allowed inside, so she got fake documents showing she was a nurse and she was able to pass into the ghetto to bring food and clothing.

By 1942, the Nazis' deadly plan became apparent. Irena surrendered even more of her security and took an even more dangerous step. She joined the resistance—the Polish underground organization Zegota. She gathered ten friends and they began a mission to rescue children, smuggling them out of the ghetto in suitcases, boxes, and even coffins. They often had to sedate the littlest ones to get them safely out. The original ten eventually grew to be twenty-four women and one man—all risking their lives for the children.

Each mission was timed and planned down to the split second to slip between patrols. The children were passed on through a network of sewers, basements, and secret passages. The work was dangerous, but one by one, Irena and her friends managed to save the lives of more than twenty-five hundred children.

In her later years, the memories that haunted her were the scenes of parents having to surrender their beloved children with no guarantee of their safety or whether they would ever see each other again. The children were placed in Catholic convents and orphanages and given non-Jewish names, but Irena kept records of each child's real name against the new name and buried these thousands of scraps of paper in glass jars in her friend's garden.

In 1943 she was captured by the Nazis and taken to prison. She was tortured but refused to name her co-conspirators or tell her captors where the jars were hidden. She faced death many times in prison until a bribed official put her name on a list of executed prisoners and let her go free. She went into hiding but continued her rescue work.

When the war was over, the little social worker dug up her jars and began the painstaking work of trying to reunite children with their families. Tragically only a few reunions were possible. Not many lived through the Holocaust. Polish families adopted some of the rescued children and others were sent to Israel.

Irena Sendler died in 2008 at the age of ninety-eight. She lived most of her life in obscurity but toward the end of her life, her story became known. She never got used to the attention. She said, "Every child saved with my help is the justification of my existence on earth and not a title to glory."[2]

LETTING GO AND LETTING GOD

Years ago I read the classic *The Christian's Secret of a Happy Life* by Hannah Whitall Smith. She tells of leaving our burdens—our troubles and worries—with God:

> Most Christians are like a man who was toiling along the road, bending under a heavy burden, when a wagon overtook him, and the driver kindly offered to help him on his journey. He joyfully accepted the offer, but when seated in the wagon, continued to bend beneath his burden, which he still kept on his shoulders. "Why don't you lay down your burden?" asked the kindhearted driver. "Oh!" replied the man, "I feel that it is almost too much to ask you to carry me, and I could not think of letting you carry my burden too." And so Christians, who have given themselves into the care and keeping of the Lord

Jesus, still continue to bend beneath the weight of their burdens, and often go weary and heavy laden throughout the whole length of their journey.[3]

THE REWARDS OF SURRENDER

Just as with so many of the other words we've considered, there are rewards promised to those who surrender. Here are just a few:

- Peace—"Do not be anxious about anything, but in every situation, by prayer and petition, with thanksgiving, present your requests to God. And the peace of God, which transcends all understanding, will guard your hearts and your minds in Christ Jesus" (Philippians 4:6–7).
- Prosperity—"Submit to God and be at peace with Him; in this way prosperity will come to you" (Job 22:21).
- Freedom—"But thanks be to God that, though you used to be slaves to sin, you have come to obey from your heart the pattern of teaching that has now claimed your allegiance" (Romans 6:17).

I think of Amy Carmichael, the legendary missionary to India. When she was twenty-four, she wrote to her mother, Catherine Carmichael, to ask if she had "given her child unreservedly to the Lord." Her mother replied:

My own precious child, yes, dearest Amy. He has lent you to me all these years. He only knows what a strength,

comfort and joy you have been to me. So, darling, when
He asks you now to go away from within my reach, can
I say no? No, Amy, He is yours—you are His—to take
where He pleases and to use you as He pleases.[4]

That is surrender.

CHOOSING YOUR WORD

You not only have to listen to God for your new word each year,
you have to also listen to the cry of your own heart. I start taking stock of my year toward the end of December, reading over
my journal entries to see where God has taken me. I look at my
goals and see where I need to go for the next year. Often my
need intersects with the whispers I've been hearing from the
Lord and my word for the year begins to take shape.

WORDPLAY

In our quest to find sensory ways to remind us of our word
throughout the year, let's not forget the sense of smell. Our
words can become sweet incense if we create a candle with
our word written on it. It's easy to paint a candle. All you
need is a brush, acrylic paint, and candle-painting medium.
You can find easy directions on the Web or at your local craft
store. Or if you don't want to paint the word, create a stencil
of the word and apply it to the candle. Once you've added
your word on the candle, let it light your quiet time, reminding you of your one perfect word.

From My Prayer Journal

Today as I celebrate my birthday, Lord, I ask that I be malleable clay in Your loving hands. Spin me, Father. Mold me. Shape me into the vibrant Christian woman You long for me to be. I desire to be a servant to Your perfect plan for my life. I hear Your voice asking me to trust You—to step forward in faith and let go! I am such a controlling person. I see my sins. I understand my faults. I pray, Father, that You can work on my stubborn heart. Make me willing to be willing. Amen.

Yes, my soul, find rest in God; my hope comes from him.
—Psalm 62:5

Thirteen

HOPE

Hope [hohp]
—noun The feeling that what is wanted can be had or that events will turn out for the best. A particular instance of this feeling: *the hope of winning.* Grounds for this feeling in a particular instance: *There is little or no hope of his recovery.*
—verb *(used with object)* To look forward to with desire and reasonable confidence. To believe, desire, or trust: *I hope that my work will be satisfactory.*

On January 1, 2006, I wrote in my journal:

The first day of the year arrives. . . . "May the God of hope fill you with all joy and peace as you trust in Him, so that you may overflow with hope by the power of the Holy Spirit." Romans 15:13

It seems each time the first day of the year arrives I become rather poetic. I look ahead at the fresh new year filled with such promise and so much hope. It's like a stash of yarn, this new year, just waiting ever so patiently to be knitted into the finest of garments—treasured sweaters or a comfortable afghan.

I've been thinking about my word for this year. God gives it to me and I simply wait for Him to reveal it to me. This year the word is hope, *a simple four-letter word. It's turning up every time I open my Bible or pick up a book to read.*

Last year, my word was wisdom, *and I certainly needed it in dealing with Mom and the trauma she endured the last months of her life. In some ways, I still have a problem believing she's gone. Oh, how I miss my mother. Very blessed I am to have had such wonderful parents and Wayne and my children.*

My life is filled with hopeful expectation for these times. Hope is a good word in other ways. I live in hope of being reunited with my parents one day. I live in hope for the promise of Jesus Christ's return in glory to claim His saints. I live in hope for losing weight and becoming the woman God always intended. Yes, hope is a very good word for me indeed.

I've always been an optimistic person, but hope is something very different. Henri Nouwen said,

Optimism and hope are radically different attitudes. Optimism is the expectation that things—the weather, human relationships, the economy, the political situation, and so on—will get better. Hope is the trust that God will fulfill God's promises to us in a way that leads us to true freedom. The optimist speaks about concrete changes in the future. The person of hope lives in the moment with the knowledge and trust that all of life is in good hands.[1]

FINDING HOPE

I love that. "All of life is in good hands." That's the hope we have in us. But how do we get that hope?

- **Hope comes from God.** Any other kind is temporary. If we have renewed hope because we finally landed a good job, we're looking for hope in all the wrong places. Lasting hope is knowing that God will take care of us whether we have that good job or not. Nothing can take that assurance away from us. No circumstance can dash our hope. "Find rest, O my soul, in God alone: my hope comes from Him" (Psalm 62:5).
- **Acknowledge that we are in good hands.** It's good to know that our future is in the hands of One who always keeps His promises. "Let us hold unswervingly to the hope we profess, for he who promised is faithful" (Hebrews 10:23).
- **Accept that we don't have control.** As Reinhold Niebuhr's famous poem says in part, "God grant me the serenity to accept the things I cannot change; courage to change the things I can; and wisdom to know the difference." And it's not just acceptance. We can take action. In chapter 12, where I talk about the word *surrender*, remember Hannah Whitall Smith's written illustrations about leaving our burdens with the Lord?

When we leave our troubles, we come away with hope. "Cast all your anxiety on him because he cares for you" (1 Peter 5:7).

- **Recognize that our time here on earth is just one chapter of our story.** If only we could see things from God's point of view, we'd worry a whole lot less and hope a whole lot more. That's one of the reasons I love the last scene from C. S. Lewis's Narnia book *The Last Battle*, where this life on earth is referred to as the Shadowlands and our lifespan is only the school term. " 'There was a real railway accident,' said Aslan softly. 'Your mother and father and all of you are—as you used to call it in the Shadowlands—dead. The term is over: the holidays have begun. The dream is ended: this is the morning.' " [2]

- **The journey is more important than the destination.** We always get so fixated on the end result that we often forget that God cares more about how we handle the journey than about how it turns out. Notice that we often refer to the Christian life in terms of something ongoing—*journey, walk, following.* We will find our hope in obedience during the process.

EACH DAY'S PECULIAR JOY

I have learned much from the life of Fanny Crosby, the beloved hymn writer who penned more than nine thousand songs in her lifetime, including "Safe in the Arms of Jesus," "Rescue the Perishing," "Blessed Assurance," and "All the Way My Savior Leads Me." One of the striking details about this prolific artist is that she was blind. "Blindness," she wrote in later life, "cannot keep the sunlight of hope from the trustful soul. One of the easiest resolves that I formed in my young and joyous heart was to leave all care to yesterday, and to believe that the morning would bring forth its own peculiar joy."

Much has been written about her as an adult, and nearly all the biographies mention that her life was marked by a deep sense of contentment. The truth is it took many years of following Jesus to bring that sweet contentment. As a child, Fanny was anything but content. Blindness in her day meant that she would never go to school, that she would never be able to read and write. Fanny refused to accept that. She longed to learn. She couldn't get enough words, ideas, and stories. By the time she was eight years old, she had memorized most of the New Testament, the five Books of the Law, Psalms, Proverbs, and the Song of Solomon.

That near-perfect memory and ability to order her thoughts became legendary. William H. Doane, one of her musical collaborators, burst into her room on April 30, 1868, and said, "There are just forty minutes before my train leaves for Cincinnati." He hummed a melody. "Can you write words for it?" Twenty minutes passed in silence broken only by the ticking of the clock, Mr. Doane waiting, Fanny Crosby thinking. Then she turned around to him. "It is all done," she said, and dictated her verses for "Safe in the Arms of Jesus." He caught his train, bearing with him words that were destined to bring comfort to thousands of people.

The stories of people who were touched and saved by the words of Fanny Crosby's songs would fill volumes. She understood suffering and the need for hope, no matter what form it took. She wrote, "Suffering is no argument of God's displeasure but a part of the fiber of our lives. I am constantly writing of hope for downcast souls."

Hope was the guiding principle of her life. She said, "Mine has been an experience that has ripened into faith as strong as the hills; it has given me a hope that admits me into the room called 'Beautiful.' "³

RESTORING LOST HOPE

When we most need hope, sometimes we can't even see it. It reminds me of the scene I wrote for my Christmas book *The Trouble with Angels*. The three angels, Shirley, Goodness, and Mercy, are sent to earth on assignment again, despite Gabriel's misgivings. Goodness has a particularly troublesome case. She's sent to a pastor, Paul Morris, who lost his wife two years earlier and just can't seem to get over it. It's caused a crisis of faith.

At one point Goodness decides to break the rules and perform a miracle to restore hope to this discouraged, grieving man. Here's how it went:

> A noise at the far end of the church attracted Goodness's attention. With no time to waste, she rushed to the manger scene and positioned herself at the appropriate spot at the peak of the stable roof.
>
> Pastor Morris walked into the sanctuary just then. Goodness closed her eyes and glowed until the glory of God's light shone through her. Heat radiated from her body. Her wings were spread to their full magnificent glory.
>
> She waited and waited.

Certain now that she'd captured Reverend Morris's attention, she opened her eyes, to discover him tucking his sermon notes into the Bible situated at the podium.

Goodness glowed brighter. The light spilled into the church, illuminating the hymnbook room like a thousand gleaming candles.

Nothing.

Paul Morris walked down the center aisle, pausing now and again to tuck a in the proper receptacle.

When Goodness couldn't stand it any longer, she called out to him in her most angelic voice. "Paul Morris."

The reverend hesitated.

"God loves you," she told him, certain hearing her say the words would revolutionize the minister's life.

Paul scratched the side of his head and turned around. It was as if he were blind. After a moment he walked over to the side door, opened it, and stuck out his head.

"Leta," he called, "did you want me for something?"

"No," came the faint reply.

Paul scratched the side of his head once more. "I could have sworn I heard my name." With that he walked out of the church.

Goodness couldn't believe it. She'd performed perhaps her greatest miracle. She'd risked Gabriel's wrath. And for what?

Paul Morris hadn't even noticed.[4]

When we get so wrapped up in our problems, like my character Reverend Paul Morris, we miss the miracles—and the hope they inspire—all around us. How do we take our eyes off the problems and listen to the voice of God?

- **Fix your thoughts.** We can control what we focus on, what we think about. Hope comes when we keep our eyes focused on the good stuff. "Finally, brothers and sisters, whatever is true, whatever is noble, whatever is right, whatever is pure, whatever is lovely, whatever is admirable—if anything is excellent or praiseworthy—think about such things. Whatever you have learned or received or heard from me, or seen in me—put it into practice. And the God of peace will be with you" (Philippians 4:8–9).
- **Make room in your life to listen.** We fill our lives up with so much noise and activity that we leave little space for God to talk to us. He says, "Be still, and know that I am God; I will be exalted among the nations, I will be exalted in the earth" (Psalm 46:10). Be still. Excellent advice.
- **Spend time soaking up hope.** The Bible is filled with verses of hope. Try to find a new one every day.

CHOOSING YOUR WORD

So far most of the words I've shared with you have grown out of my own walk with God and could be considered "spiritual." Don't be surprised if God wants to explore a word that isn't necessarily spiritual. As I write this, my word for this year is *listen*. Hmm. Do you think God is trying to tell me something? I am trying to listen more and talk less. You might be assigned the word *laughter* at some point. Or *feast*. Or *creativity*. Just remember, there is no dividing line in God's world with one side marked spiritual and other earthly. It's all sacred and it's all earthly at the same time.

WORDPLAY

One of my friends told me of a family who took the Bible literally. They painted God's words on the doorposts of their home (Deuteronomy 11:20). It's certainly a conversation starter. But many designers use word stencils to decorate walls. If you have a place that's yours alone, you might want to consider stenciling your words on the wall as a beautiful reminder of your one perfect word.

From My Prayer Journal

Breathe into me, heavenly Father, hope to strive forward so that I might be all that You intended. Just as You placed that instinct in birds to migrate toward the summer sunshine, place that godly instinct in me so that I might soar straight into the arms of Your will without forethought or knowledge. Amen.

Whatever you do, work at it with all your heart,
as working for the Lord, not for human masters.
—Colossians 3:23

Fourteen

PASSION

Pas·sion [*pa*-shuhn]
—noun Any powerful or compelling emotion or feeling, as love or hate.

On January 1, 2007, I opened my journal with these words:

Every new year is filled with expectation and hope. How like our Lord Jesus to build into our lives fresh opportunities, another chance in place to put the past behind us and to strive anew.

Earlier I read the opening pages of my 2006 journal and compared the unlived year to a room full of yarn yet to be knitted. The analogy was a good one. This year, 2007, is 365 days yet to be lived—yet to be traveled.

Last year, my word for the year was hope. *I felt that that word came at me in a number of different ways until it was such an obvious choice. As I prayed for my word for this year, I considered and discarded a number of ideas. God's leading was subtle. I finally decided on* passion.

I'm a passionate person, passionate about Christ and His Word in my life, passionate about my family, my husband, children, and grandchildren. I'm passionate about my books, my career, my friends and business relationships.

As soon as I thought of passion, *the word immediately felt right. All the areas of my life that I've mentioned demand passion and that's my intent for this year.*

Passion. Yes, that word fits me to a T. I've never been able to be cool. Ask me about my next story and it will come tumbling out. I can't help myself. If the conversation moves on to grandchildren, oh my goodness, stop me, someone! The same with cooking. Knitting. My family. Jesus.

The Trouble with Cool

But I'm not going to apologize. It is important to approach life with passion. In Revelation 3:15–16, God says, "I know your deeds, that you are neither cold nor hot. I wish you were either one or the other! So, because you are lukewarm—neither hot nor cold—I am about to spit you out of my mouth."

Yikes! We don't want to be spit out because of our lack of passion. *Lukewarm* is just another word for what our society calls "cool." We value coolness. Be cool. Withhold excess emotion. Move through life with an ironic detachment, a distance, an absence of excitement. There has been a carefully cultivated aristocratic cool called *sprezzatura* for centuries. In 1508, Baldassare Castiglione began writing *The Book of the Courtier*, a guidebook to etiquette, so to speak, in Renaissance court life. He originated the word *sprezzatura*. Sprezzatura has been described as "the ability to disguise what one really desires, feels, thinks, and means or intends behind a mask of apparent reticence and nonchalance."[1] In his guidebook, he even encouraged the courtier to cultivate an air of ease in accomplishing difficult actions that hid the conscious effort that went into realizing them. In other words, don't let them see you sweat. Doesn't it sound like our modern version of "cool"?

With the help of film and media, we've come to value the aesthetic of cool. Our children work hard to gain peer approval by appearing cool. We try to mask our enthusiasm in order to cultivate a sense of control at work. Sometimes we even approach travel and adventure with a veneer of ennui, a jaded "been there, done that" attitude. Like the Ogden Nash tongue-in-cheek poem, "I would live all my life in nonchalance and insouciance / Were it not for making a living, which is rather a nouciance."

But what does God think about cool?

I believe it is disgusting to Him. We spit disgusting things out of our mouths, don't we? The adjective *deceptively* is often applied to the noun *cool*. "He appeared deceptively cool." Since being cool, or sprezzatura, is carefully cultivated, it is nothing short of deception, right? It's acting.

Part of the reason the Lord loves little children so much is that there is little artifice in them. What you see is what you get. They are honest, often to their parents' dismay. A little child is not jaded. He sees the world through fresh eyes and is passionate about it. I wonder if that is why we're told to come to faith as a little child.

Passion is the opposite of cool. If cool is bad in the Lord's eyes, we need to embrace the passion He has planted in all of us.

Passion Subdued and Expressed

In Isak Dinesen's beloved story "Babette's Feast," I find the themes of passion explored in fascinating ways—passion lavished and passion restrained.

The story opens in the town of Berlevaag on the coast of Norway, in the home of the pastor of an aging congregation—a remnant who faithfully follows his own self-styled, strict Lutheran sect. The dean, as he was called, lived with his two middle-aged daughters: Martine, named after Martin Luther, and Philippa, named after Luther's friend and biographer.

Both daughters had been extraordinary beauties in their youth. When Martine was eighteen, she'd caught the eye of the dashing Lorens Loewenhielm, a young lieutenant who was the nephew of one of the congregants. Everyone acknowledged he had great prospects but being around Martine made him feel diminished. It was like having a mirror held up until all he could see were his libertine ways. It made him ashamed. He felt profoundly unworthy, so rather than declare his love, he kissed Martine's hand and announced that he would never see her again. He left and made himself a promise that he would become a great military leader so that he would never feel lacking again.

Philippa had an exceptional singing voice, though she only sang for the little congregation. The renowned Paris opera singer Achille Papin happened to be visiting their town and heard her sing in church. Her voice reignited his passion for music and ended the ennui from which he'd been suffering. He knew, with her exquisite soprano voice, she could be the talk of every salon in Paris. The dean allowed him to give Philippa voice lessons and Papin continued to build his dream of introducing her to the stage. After one impromptu duet, carried away by the music, he impulsively kissed her—meaning nothing by the kiss. Philippa could not view it in the same light. She turned down his offer of potential renown and asked her father to write to him, telling him she would not see him again.

Both passionate but thwarted men left and the sisters settled into their quiet life in Berlevaag.

Eventually the dean died and his daughters carried on in his memory, caring for the faithful few in their church. Unfortunately bickering and infighting marred the once-gentle relationships of the people.

Fifteen years later a letter arrived from Papin in Paris, carried by a woman dressed in tattered clothing. Monsieur Papin wrote that he had never forgotten the sisters' warm hospitality and he asked if they would accept Babette Hersant, who lost her husband and son in an uprising in Paris, as a housekeeper. He ended his letter by saying, "She can cook."

The kind sisters took Babette in despite their misgivings. She was Catholic, after all, and only spoke French—an unsettling combination. They managed to explain to her that they had no money and could not pay her, but she was happy to work in exchange for a place to live. Papin's letter had indicated that Babette could cook, but taking nothing for granted, the sisters patiently taught her to cook the plain fare they ate—porridge and simple soups. She quietly took over care of the sisters and their dwindling congregation for fourteen years—always in the background, always somewhat foreign and mysterious.

Her one tie to her native Paris was her lottery ticket that a friend renewed for her each year. Just as the little congregation, now down to a handful of aged souls, was preparing a celebration in honor of what would have been the dean's hundredth birthday, Babette received word that she had won the prize of ten thousand francs in the lottery. The sisters fully expected her to use the money to leave, perhaps to go back home to Paris in style. They had come to have a deep affection for her and could hardly bear the thought of losing her.

When Babette came to speak to them, they braced themselves to hear that she would be leaving. They were surprised when, instead, she asked if they would allow her to pay for and prepare a French dinner in honor of the dean's birthday. The sisters were reluctant, but because Babette had never asked them for anything in all her years of service, they agreed.

Babette asked for leave to go to France to buy the ingredients she would need to cook the meal. When she returned she was animated—a new person. A few weeks later supplies—bottles and strange cheeses, herbs and meats—began to arrive at the house. Most disconcerting of all, a live giant turtle was delivered.

The sisters became increasingly anxious about the meal. How would the congregation feel about the foreign food, the strange ingredients? They decided to talk to them about it, explaining that they were allowing the meal out of kindness for a faithful servant. They asked the church members to overlook any discomfort and to be gracious. The usually bickering flock agreed because they loved Philippa and Martine.

The stage was set. Babette had hired help in the kitchen and she prepared and cooked for days. She even unpacked delicate tableware she'd purchased in Paris and set a table sparkling with snowy linens, candles, china, and crystal.

The morning of the celebration the sisters received a note from Mrs. Loewenhielm saying that she would be bringing her nephew, General Loewenhielm. Martine informed Babette there would be one more for dinner—a man who had lived many years in Paris. Babette was delighted.

The congregation assembled and sang a hymn together, feeling more connected than they had in years. Martine reminded them one last time that Babette worked very hard on the meal and even if it was not to their liking, they should say nothing about the food or drink.

On the drive to the dean's house, the general reflected on the unparalleled success he'd made of his life—his military career, beautiful wife, and financial success. He could not understand why he was not satisfied. He thought back to his visit with the dean when he was a dissolute young officer. He'd attained all he wanted to attain, had even supped with kings, but what about his soul?

When all were gathered at the table and the blessing had been spoken, Babette's assistant began to serve the food and wine. Course after exquisite course came out, beginning with an amontillado and *potage à la tortue* and finishing with *savarin au rhum avec des figues et fruits glacés*, including an 1845 Clos de Vougeot.

The general was astonished by the wines and foods, the quality of which he hadn't seen since his old Paris days, and yet the guests didn't even comment on the food. He was perplexed. It was as if they ate this fare—fare for royalty—every day. Finally overcome, he stood up to deliver a speech about bliss and righteousness. The congregation gathered around the table understood little of what he said but were moved by the passion and eloquence. In the warmth of the evening all the old grudges and petty hurts melted away. As they all prepared to leave, the general took Martine's hand and told her that he'd never forgotten her. They parted in friendship, finally appreciating the effect their long-ago meeting had had on the rest of their lives.

The sisters walked into the kitchen to thank their maid for her gift of the meal. With a mountain of dirty dishes surrounding her, Babette was pensive. She admitted she was once the chef at the finest restaurant in all of Paris, the Café Anglais. The sisters listened. Babette had never shared about the life she led before she appeared on their doorstep. They had little point of reference to understand what that meant, but they asked, now that she had money, if she planned to go back to Paris. Babette said she would never go back—the Paris she once knew was gone. The restaurants were gone and the people who appreciated her food were also gone. Besides, she said, she couldn't go back because she had no money. She had spent the entire fortune on that one meal.

The plainspoken sisters were speechless. They could not fathom how one meal could cost ten thousand francs and that now Babette was penniless. Babette waved off their sympathy as she told them that "the artist is never poor," explaining that she was a great artist and she needed to prepare that meal to express her art one more time.

Philippa, the sister who could have been one of the greatest sopranos in Europe, embraced Babette with new understanding. She told Babette that her art would not be lost because in paradise she would be all God meant her to be.[2]

Babette is a Christ figure of sorts in the story. She gives of herself extravagantly even if those who receive the gift don't understand the value of it. Christ's sacrifice for us is often called "the passion of Christ." It's one of the reasons I could read this story and watch the film version over and over again. There are so many themes and so many layers. I feel as if I might not ever quite get to the bottom of it.

I understand the passion Babette felt for food and cooking. Not just because I love cooking but because it mirrors the way I feel about storytelling and writing. I have to keep myself in balance or I would write to the exclusion of everything else.

When Philippa declares that Babette will someday express her art in heaven, I want to applaud. I will also write books in heaven. On August 27, 1998, I wrote the following prayer:

Dear Lord, it's been nearly fifteen years ago now that You spoke to my heart in prayer and reminded me that there were wonderful books in heaven You had for me to write. Ever since that moment I have been incredibly excited about heaven and eternal life. My heart longs for the next life as well as enjoying this one. Amen.

EMBRACING OUR PASSION

We need to find our passion, act on it, and openly share it. We have to take this in two steps. First we need to recognize that we were created to be passionate. To embrace life. We need to cultivate this by stripping away the artifice and control we've carefully created over the years. I think Jenny Joseph's poem "Warning," which begins, "When I am an old woman I shall wear purple," addresses this. We need to fight coolness with every fiber of our being. I want to stop admiring the cool, the detached people. I want to hug the messy, conflicted, honest, passionate people who are living their lives with enthusiasm.

As I write this, I understand that someone reading this book may be expending so much energy battling feelings of sadness, loss, anger, or frustration that she can barely get her head off the pillow, let alone embrace life with passion. I've stood alongside people I love who've battled clinical depression. I hate the disease. The good news is there are treatments for depression that can often get a person back on an even keel—ready to tackle things like rediscovering the passion in life. If the detachment you are feeling is not a "carefully cultivated cool," consider that you might need a helping hand before you can take the next step. God wants you well. He said so in 2 Timothy 1:7—"For God hath not given us the spirit of fear; but of power, and of love, and of a sound mind." (KJV)

FINDING YOUR OWN PASSION

Once we've rediscovered our passionate nature, we need to find our passion—find what God created us to do. When I talk about my passion for writing I invariably meet someone who will say, "I wish I knew what I was supposed to do with my life."

The hints are all there. It's already been percolating in you all these years. You just need to recognize it. I could write a whole book on this subject, but let me give you a few techniques for discovering your own passion.

1. **What invokes your feeling of *Sehnsucht*?** I talked about this idea in chapter 4, when I explored my word *hunger*. *Sehnsucht* is the word C. S. Lewis used to describe that inconsolable longing, that deep feeling of connection that can't really be explained by any word in the

English language. The first time I put words to my dream of becoming a writer was when Sister Anna Maureen called me to the office at Saint Joseph Academy during my senior year to ask the question asked of everyone in the graduating class: what do you want to do after graduation?

"I'm going to write books," I told her, and promptly burst into tears. I'd never formally put my dream into words. I'm guessing the poor sister had never had that reaction before. She patted me on the back and called my mother to come pick me up. I'm surprised she didn't administer an aspirin or two.

Had I not already known what my passion was, that would have been a dead giveaway. My friend always says that when we cry at a story or a song or an idea, we need to explore it further. It's a sign of *sehnsucht.* It's an indication the Holy Spirit is talking to us.

2. **What one desire have you never put in words?** If it's a dream you're almost afraid to put in words, there's a good chance this is a God-given passion. If we were able to sit down together and I asked you, "Tell me one thing you'd love to do that is so big and so scary, you've never told anyone else," what would you tell me? Chances are, that's your passion.

3. **Make a list.** Do a quick exercise to help uncover your passions. I say *quick* because writing fast and furious gets past the editor in your brain and helps reveal things you'd normally edit out.

   • First make a list of all the things you'd love to do if you had all the time, money, and support you needed. Quickly. Write fast until you have twenty of them.

- Now look at that list and pick five that resonate—that seem big and revealing. For each one, answer the question "What's stopping me?" Write down all the reasons it seems impossible.
- Pick one or two of those dreams and write a solution for each roadblock. Let's say you answered that you'd like to start a foundation to build wells in Africa, knowing that clean water close to their homes and fields ends hunger and poverty for a whole village. That's a big dream. On your roadblock list you might have written, "I don't even have money for next month's rent, let alone Africa." Valid point, but what about applying for grants? Are you good at speaking and selling your dream? Could you enlist partners to help you reach your goal? Do you work for a corporate entity that likes to put money behind causes proposed by employees? Look for solutions instead of focusing on the problems. You can counter every challenge you can conjure up.

Play with this exercise long before you talk with naysayers. Finding your passion is the first step toward putting legs to your dreams. If somebody had told me that publishing was hard to break into and that most writers are fortunate if they have one or two books with modest sales, who knows what that would have done to my dream?

I hope you find your passion and kick over every roadblock in order to achieve your dream. As Frederick Buechner said: "The place God calls you to is the place where your deep gladness and the world's deep hunger meet."[3]

CHOOSING YOUR WORD

In this chapter we talked about passion. Don't overlook your own passions and preferences in choosing the word you want to discover. Those interests may have been planted by the Lord deep inside you and are part of listening for His voice. If you love gardening and the outdoors, for instance, and can't wait until each season changes so you can see the world through a new seasonal filter, do you think the Lord might be drawing you toward a word like *creation? Seasons? Rebirth?* We have to fully accept the way God made us in order to find out what He wants us to explore.

WORDPLAY

If you've read any of my books, you know Christmas is my favorite time of the year. I'm like a little child. There's nothing I want to celebrate more than the birth of my Savior. I won't even tell you how many nativity scenes I take out at Christmas, nor will I tell you how many trees we trim. But oh, how the house sparkles with the celebration! It stands to reason that I plan to find Christmas ornaments to represent every word I've had over the years. As I unwrap the ornaments each year I'm reminded of when I got the ornament, where it came from, and what it represents. One perfect word ornament will be a perfect medium for remembering what I've learned.

From My Prayer Journal

Oh Father, my soul and my heart pound with love, for You so loved me that You gave Your Son so that I might have life. I praise You and thank You. I am determined to live my life in a way that honors You. Instead of worrying about what the future holds . . . I will rest in Your arms. Each day help me to practice love and joy. Remind me of the benefits of laughter and give me a reason to laugh. Let me sing You a new song. Amen.

"For I know the plans I have for you," declares
the LORD, *"plans to prosper you and not to harm
you, plans to give you hope and a future."*
—Jeremiah 29:11

Fifteen

PURPOSE

Pur·pose [*pur*-puhs]
—noun The reason for which something exists or is done, made, used, etc. An intended or desired result; end; aim; goal. Determination; resoluteness.
—verb (*used with object*) To set as an aim, intention, or goal for oneself. To intend; design. To resolve (to do something): *He purposed to change his way of life radically.*

I've always wanted to be a woman of purpose. As Helen Keller said, "Many persons have the wrong idea of what constitutes true happiness. It is not attained through self-gratification but through fidelity to a worthy purpose."[1]

Or as Rick Warren puts it on the first page of his book *The Purpose Driven Life*, "It's not about you."[2]

God created all of us to worship Him, but He gave each one of us specific gifts. And in many, many ways, He's given us a multitude of talents and it's how we choose to focus those that defines how we will fulfill our purpose.

I know God has called me to be a writer—a storyteller. I always think of what Eric Liddell, the runner, said in the film *Chariots of Fire:* "I believe God made me for a purpose, but He also made me fast. And when I run I feel His pleasure."

I could say the same thing. I believe God made me for a purpose, but He also made me a passionate storyteller. When I write I feel His pleasure.

There have been two times in my career where I've had to make a decision to be a writer. I used to host a radio show every Friday morning with fellow author Linda Lael Miller. The show became so popular that we were approached about doing a nationally syndicated show. This was heady stuff—the big time. I had to decide if I was a writer or if I was a radio personality. And my love—my purpose—is telling stories and writing, so I turned it down. Since that first opportunity, I've been asked twice more to do a syndicated radio show. It's a good thing I examined my purpose early on.

Another skill is speaking. I love being a speaker, whether to a small group, from a podium, or to an entire ballroom of people. I believe God's given me a talent in that area. I probably could make a living as a speaker. But do I want to speak, or do I want to write? That's easy. I want to be a writer. I know this is what God intended for me and what makes me happiest.

God's Purpose for Us

I read in the book *Simple Little Words* about how sometimes God's purpose is entirely different from our own.

Edna Ellison had one goal in mind: Her daughter's wedding was going to be perfect. Like most mothers-of-the-bride, she had planned for months, organizing every detail with drill-sergeant precision.

She wished her husband was still alive to enjoy this special moment in their daughter's life, and she missed his broad shoulders as she carried the weight of the responsibility alone.

The wedding day neared and Edna met with the floral designer to discuss the final details for decorating the church. "Edna, why don't we use fresh greenery and magnolia blossoms for the front of the sanctuary?" the florist suggested. "You can probably find a magnolia tree in your neighborhood, and it will save you some money. We'll decorate the day before the wedding, and then we can turn the air-conditioning really low so the blossoms will stay fresh until after the ceremony."

Edna agreed. After they decorated the sanctuary, the church looked beautiful as Edna had imagined it in her dreams.

The next morning, Edna and her future son-in-law arrived at the church. The temperature that day was a blazing 107 degrees. Upon opening the church doors, a blast of hot air hit them instead of the refreshing coolness they had expected. They discovered that a storm during the night had knocked the power out and the air-conditioning had been off.

Edna entered the sanctuary and was horrified to see that the once glossy white magnolia blossoms were now wilted and black.

She panicked. Turning to her future son-in-law, she said, "What will we do? We can't have people come to a wedding with black flowers—and we only have a few hours until the ceremony!"

"Drive around and find whatever flowers you can and bring them back."

Edna drove through the neighborhood surrounding the church and finally saw a magnolia tree in the distance. She pulled in the driveway, rushed from the car, and knocked frantically on the door.

When an elderly man answered, she blurted, "I need you." She quickly shared the wedding-disaster story.

The eighty-six-year-old man grabbed a step stool; then he cut the blossoms and handed them to Edna. She thanked him profusely.

As she turned to leave, he said, "You don't realize what just happened here."

She looked at him quizzically. Tears welled in his eyes as he explained, "My wife died on Monday. Tuesday night, we received friends at the funeral home down the road." A trail of tears trickled down his wrinkled cheeks. "We buried her on Wednesday, and on Friday, all my children went home."

He struggled to get the next words out. Edna grasped his hand, waiting for him to finish.

"Now it's just me, and the house is so empty. I fed my wife every bite the last few years, and she doesn't need me anymore. My children are gone and they don't need me, either. I feel so alone. Right before you came, I shook my fist at God and shouted, 'God, does anybody need me?' As the words left my mouth, you knocked on the door and the exact words you said were, 'I need you.'"

In a halting voice, he continued, "While I was cutting the magnolia blossoms for you, it dawned on me that maybe I can have a flower ministry. I noticed at the fu-

neral home that some of the caskets didn't have flowers.
I could take some for them. And maybe I can take some
flowers to people at the nursing homes and hospitals to
help brighten their days."

Edna wiped the tears from her cheeks, overwhelmed
as she realized that God had fine-tuned the details of *her*
child's wedding day so that one of *his* hurting children
could hear the words "I need you." *

Each one of us needs a purpose in life. And we all need to
move through life with purpose. For me, the year was 2008
and my word was *purpose*. Here's how I opened that year in my
journal:

> *Tuesday—a whole new year of 2008. The possibilities
> are boundless, a fresh year filled with expectations. I'm
> always eager to look ahead. I love fresh starts, and I'm
> grateful You placed them in our lives. Fresh starts—Your
> promises are fresh every morning. This, however, is a
> special day, the start of a new year. I give this year to You,
> Father, and all that it may hold, content to offer it up
> to You.*

FOR SUCH A TIME AS THIS

The story of Esther from the Bible is the story of purpose. She
was chosen "for such a time as this."

Let me tell the story. Once upon a time the king Xerxes gave

---

* Michelle Cox and John Perrodin, *Simple Little Words* (Colorado Springs: David C. Cook, 2008), 25.

a lavish party. He ordered Vashti, the queen, to make an appearance wearing her crown so that everyone could see how beautiful she was. Some Bible scholars believe that the crown was all the king wanted her to wear. She refused and it infuriated Xerxes. The king's advisers believed that by her disobedience she set a terrible example. They worried that all their women would follow suit and disobey their husbands. The king, who was easily influenced, banished Vashti from his presence forever. He decided to sponsor a beauty pageant of sorts to find her replacement.

Mordecai was a Jew who lived in the palace and was part of the Persian bureaucracy under Xerxes. When his young cousin Hadassah, who went by the name of Esther, was orphaned, Mordecai took her under his care and became her adopted father. Esther's beauty was legendary, so he brought her to the palace to compete for the king's favor. Mordecai insisted, however, that she hide her connection to him. Esther outshone all the other girls and became a favorite of the harem master. Though she joined the other hopefuls in the harem she was assigned seven maids to care for her and she and her entourage were given the finest quarters in the harem. Esther began an intensive yearlong regimen with special foods, complicated beauty treatments, exotic cosmetics, and costly perfumes.

When the time came for Esther to be presented to the king, she pleased him above all the others and he declared her queen. He gave a lavish banquet in her honor and proclaimed a holiday throughout the land.

Intrigue was always part of court and not long after she ascended to the throne, Esther helped Mordecai gain the king's trust by foiling an assassination plot she overheard. She had continued to keep her relationship with Mordecai a secret. No one even knew that she was a Jew. Mordecai insisted she keep that a secret as well. Mordecai's deed saving the king's life was written in the annals.

One of the king's noblemen, Haman, was singled out by the king for special honor and elevated to second in command of the Persian Empire. The king required all the noblemen at the king's gate to kneel down and pay homage to Haman. Mordecai, who would kneel to no one but the one true God, refused, which infuriated Haman, especially when he discovered Mordecai was a Jew.

Haman hated the Jews. Rather than just get even with Mordecai, he designed a plan to annihilate all the Jews. And the king, who was easily led, absentmindedly agreed, neglecting to get any details. Thus an edict of the king went out, which could not be overturned, stating that on the thirteenth day of Adar (the seventh of March by today's calendar) all Jews—men, women, and children—would be killed. Just like that.

Great mourning went out among all the Jews. There seemed to be no hope.

Mordecai put on sackcloth and ashes in mourning. He sent word to Esther to intercede for her people. When she got his message she hesitated.

She sent word back to Mordecai, saying, "All the king's officials and the people of the royal provinces know that for any man or woman who approaches the king in the inner court without being summoned the king has but one law: that they be put to death unless the king extends the gold scepter to them and spares their lives. But thirty days have passed since I was called to go to the king."

When Esther's words were reported to Mordecai, he sent back this answer: "Do not think that because you are in the king's house you alone of all the Jews will escape. For if you remain silent at this time, relief and deliverance for the Jews will arise from another place, but you and your father's family will perish. And who knows but that you have come to your royal position for such a time as this?"

Then Esther sent this reply to Mordecai: "Go, gather together all the Jews who are in Susa, and fast for me. Do not eat or drink for three days, night or day. We will fast as you do. When this is done, I will go to the king, even though it is against the law. And if I perish, I perish."

Queen Esther dressed as carefully as she ever had and came into the court not knowing if it was to be her last act. But she found favor in the king's eyes. He not only held out his scepter to her but offered to give her anything—up to half of his kingdom. She asked only that she be allowed to prepare a banquet for him and for Haman that very day.

At the banquet, the king repeated his offer and Esther asked that the king and Haman come to another banquet the next day. She promised she would then answer his question.

The evil Haman left the presence of the king and queen elated. On his way home he encountered Mordecai in the town square. Mordecai still stubbornly refused to bow down to him, even after all that had occurred. This infuriated Haman all the more. When he got home, he couldn't help boasting about all that he had accomplished. After all, he was the only one invited by the queen to not one but two banquets. But he admitted that he found no satisfaction as long as Mordecai withheld his respect. Haman's friends and family suggested that he ask the king's permission to kill Mordecai. Because Haman was so confident that the king would see it his way, he had a pole set seventy-five feet high, right in front of his house, on which to impale Mordecai. He must have found great satisfaction looking at that pole and picturing his enemy dangling on it.

On the night before Esther's second banquet, King Xerxes couldn't sleep, so he had one of his servants read to him from the Annals of the King. And it just so happened that the man read about Mordecai's uncovering the plot to assassinate him. Xerxes asked his servant if Mordecai had been rewarded, and the servant replied that he had not. This oversight disturbed the king, and he set out to fix the problem. Xerxes asked, "Who is in the court?" Haman had just arrived, intending to ask if he could have Mordecai impaled, so the king invited him in.

Without saying whom he wanted to honor, Xerxes asked Haman, "What should be done with the man that the king delights to honor?"

Haman, being rather full of himself, thought, *Who would the king delight to honor more than me?* He suggested an elaborate plan that included robes, horses, crowns, and a nobleman of the king leading the honored recipient around the city, proclaiming, "Thus it shall be done to the man whom the king delights to honor."

Xerxes liked the idea so much that he sent Haman to immediately do all just as he described—for Mordecai!

After the humiliation of having to honor Mordecai, Haman was summoned by the king's eunuchs to come to Esther's second banquet. During the feast, the king reassured Esther for the third time in two days that whatever she requested, he would do it for her. Esther, knowing that it was now or never, asked that she and her people might be saved from destruction and annihilation. When the king asked, "Who is he that might annihilate you?" Esther replied, "This vile Haman."

Furious, the king bolted from the room, leaving Haman begging for his life at the mercy of the queen. In the process, he touched her while she sat on her couch, and as he was doing this, the king returned. For this serious violation of decency and harem etiquette, Haman was immediately sentenced to death.

The king, at the urging of Esther, eventually signed a new decree and the Jews were spared.

What a powerful story of purpose—of a woman who was placed in her unique position "for such a time as this."

When we consider our own purpose, we need to explore what God called us to do that no one else can do. God made Esther extraordinarily beautiful, not for vanity's sake, but because he had a special purpose in mind for her that required physical beauty.

Like Esther, we've been chosen to fulfill a unique purpose "for such a time as this." I wouldn't have complained if I'd been chosen for a job that required exquisite beauty. God saw fit to make me a storyteller instead. He knows what He's doing. There's nothing I like better.

In chapter 14 we talked about discovering your passion. The Lord often plants the very passion in us that equips us to fulfill His purpose. Our goal is to discover that purpose. Ask a few close friends or family members what they see as your distinctive gifts, passion, and abilities. Compile a list. As you seek to discover the purpose for your life, keep that list nearby. Chances are it's filled with clues that will help you figure out who you are under God and the reason you were created.

CHOOSING YOUR WORD

Throughout the pages of this book we've talked about how you choose your word and how you explore it. Here are the key elements:

1. Listen to God and listen to your heart and choose your word.
2. Spend time in *the* Word.
3. Spend time exploring your word.
4. Record what you learn, looking at your word in light of what's happening in your life.
5. Keep your word in front of you 365 days a year.
6. At the end of the year, take stock and plan for a brand-new adventure.

WORDPLAY

Being a book person, I'm fascinated by the art of altered books. This is the craft of taking old, usually damaged, leather-bound books and changing them into entirely new books. You can find examples of this art online and you will find how-to books on the craft in art stores and bookstores. Then decide: do you do one book a year for each word or do you create one book for a lifetime of words? Once again, you'll be creating a tactile, visual treasure to represent your journey exploring one perfect word.

From My Prayer Journal

Her children rise up and call her blessed. That is the kind of woman I long to be, Lord—a blessing to my family, a blessing to my church, a blessing to the community, and a blessing to my husband. That is my goal, Father— all only achievable when I remain in You. Amen.

If you remain in me and my words remain in you,
ask whatever you wish, and it will be done for you.
—John 15:7

Sixteen

A WORD TO THE WISE

Let me end this book by giving you some advice born of my own experience. I don't claim to have the prescription for you, but I know that as I've chosen words to live by, I've experienced blessings beyond anything I could have ever imagined. Henry David Thoreau said, "If one advances confidently in the direction of his dreams, and endeavors to live the life which he has imagined, he will meet with a success unexpected in common hours." My own success was certainly unexpected in the common hours but God is not restricted to common hours.

You've probably noticed that many of the Bible verses I chose to open each chapter come with a promise attached. Look at these again:

- If you remain in me and my words remain in you, ask whatever you wish, and it will be done for you. (John 15:7)
- Jesus said to her, "I am the resurrection and the life. The one who believes in me will live, even though they

die; and whoever lives by believing in me will never die. Do you believe this?" (John 11:25–26)

- The LORD is close to the brokenhearted and saves those who are crushed in spirit. (Psalm 34:18)
- May he give you the desire of your heart and make all your plans succeed. (Psalm 20:4)
- Then Jesus declared, "I am the bread of life. Whoever comes to me will never go hungry, and whoever believes in me will never be thirsty. (John 6:35)
- Blessed is the one who trusts in the LORD, whose confidence is in him. They will be like a tree planted by the water that sends out its roots by the stream. It does not fear when heat comes; its leaves are always green. It has no worries in a year of drought and never fails to bear fruit. (Jeremiah 17:7–8)
- But if anyone obeys his word, love for God is truly made complete in them. This is how we know we are in him. (1 John 2:5)
- And without faith it is impossible to please God, because anyone who comes to him must believe that he exists and that he rewards those who earnestly seek him. (Hebrews 11:6)
- If any of you lacks wisdom, you should ask God, who gives generously to all without finding fault, and it will be given to you. (James 1:5)
- Trust in the LORD with all your heart and lean not on your own understanding; in all your ways submit to him, and he will make your paths straight. (Proverbs 3:5–6)
- "For I know the plans I have for you," declares the LORD, "plans to prosper you and not to harm you, plans to give you hope and a future." (Jeremiah 29:11)

If we do these things, God promises to give us what we ask for, He tells us we will never die, that He will save us when we are brokenhearted, that we will never be hungry or thirsty, that we will never fail to bear fruit, that His love will be made complete in us, that He will reward us for seeking Him, He'll give us wisdom if we ask, He'll make our path straight, He'll prosper us and give us hope and a future.

That's a pretty impressive list of rewards, right? And that's just a small sampling of the promises in the Bible.

In his book *How to Pray*, theologian R. A. Torrey said, "If we are to obtain from God all that we ask from Him, Christ's words must abide or continue in us. We must study His words, fairly devour His words, let them sink into our thought and into our heart, keep them in our memory, obey them constantly in our life, let them shape and mold our daily life and our every act." [1]

What great advice. "If we are to obtain from God all that we ask," we need to let Christ's words sink deep into us. How do we do that? Let's break it down.

STUDY HIS WORD

I pick one perfect word each year but I do that *in addition to* reading and studying His Word. If one word is the micro-study, reading the Bible is the macro-study. We need to understand our words in context. Set aside time each day to read the Bible. I'd recommend that you set up a reading plan or use one that has already been developed. Some people use what I heard one person call "the Lucky Dip," where you open the Bible at random and start reading there. I prefer a more planned approach. *The One Year Bible* might be a good place to start. Or use one of the many Bible reading plans you can find online, like "The 52–Week Bible Reading Plan" at www.bible-reading.com/bible -plan.html or one of the many plans at Bible Gateway (www .biblegateway.com/resources/readingplans/).

The late rabbi Dr. Herbert Opalek, who became a Christian after having been an Orthodox rabbi for more than half his life, used to say that the difference between Christians and Jews is that Christians worship God with music, Jews worship God by study.

MEDITATE ON THE WORD

When we choose a word for the year, we practice a form of meditation by spending 365 days pondering its meaning. But as we read the Bible we need to meditate as well. This means to think and pray about a certain passage. There's a Latin term, *lectio divina*, meaning "holy reading," to explain how we meditate on God's Word. The practice invites us to study, ponder, listen, pray, maybe even sing over a passage or a word. We need to take time, be still, and let God's Word sink deep into our souls.

HIDE HIS WORDS IN YOUR HEART

On September 3, 1998, I wrote the following prayer:

> *Dearest Father, nearly thirteen years ago I made the decision to memorize scripture. A verse a week. Three, sometimes four verses a month. A chapter a year. My Christian life, indeed my entire life changed from that moment forward. I can never doubt the changes this simple practice has brought into my life.*

May I always allow Your words to abide in my heart and my soul. Amen.

I invite you to do the same. You will be changed.

Pray His Words Back to Him

That sounds strange, doesn't it? Why would we pray the Bible back to the One who wrote it? In *The One Year Book of Praying Through the Bible*, Cheri Fuller says,

> As I prayed God's Word, I was filled with confidence and faith in God's ability to answer and to act because I wasn't praying out of my own understanding or imagination but out of the Lord's heart, and His intentions and desires for us, His people. As I prayed God's Word, fear, doubt, and discouragement left, and His peace renewed my heart and my mind. I discovered the Bible contained promises concerning God's plans for our lives, for our children and loved ones and the body of Christ, the provision He has available and what He has in store for us both in this life and in the life to come. He wants us to pray these promises and verses, meditate on them, and trust in the Author's ability to move on our behalf.[2]

Words are powerful. I encourage you to find one perfect word for each year. It seems like such a simple thing, but it will enrich your life in ways you could never have expected.

From My Prayer Journal

Lord, I love my job with every fiber of my being. My struggle is to remember that You are the one who gave me a writer's heart and it's important that everything I pen gives You the glory. May I never become so caught up in my own words that I lose sight of the One who created the Word! Amen.

READ MORE

Operation Auca and the lives of the five Ecuadorian missionaries.

Read:
- *Through Gates of Splendor* by Elisabeth Elliot
- *Jungle Pilot* by Russell T. Hitt
- *End of the Spear* by Steve Saint

Watch on DVD:
- *The End of the Spear*
- *Beyond the Gates of Splendor*

Anne Beiler, Jonas Beiler, and Auntie Anne's Pretzels:

Read:
- *Twist of Faith: The Story of Anne Beiler* by Anne Beiler with Shawn Smucker
- *Think No Evil* by Jonas Beiler with Shawn Smucker

NOTES

One

1. All definitions adapted from *The American Heritage Dictionary of the English Language* (New York: Houghton Mifflin, 2006) and Dictionary.com.
2. http://www.snopes.com/language/literary/greenegg.asp
3. Gilbert Keith Chesterton, *Orthodoxy* (New York: Image Books, Doubleday, Inc., 1959), 130.

Two

1. Marianne Williamson, *A Return to Love: Reflections on the Principles of "A Course in Miracles"* (New York: HarperCollins, 1996), chapter 7, section 3.

Three

1. Madeleine L'Engle, *Madeleine L'Engle Herself*, comp. Carol F. Chase (Colorado Springs: Shaw Books, Waterbrook Press, 2001), 58.
2. C. S. Lewis, *The Quotable Lewis*, eds. Wayne Martindale and Jerry Root (Wheaton, IL: Tyndale House Publishers, 1989), excerpt 91.
3. *Pentecostal Evangel*, December 9, 2001, http://www.ag.org/pentecostal-evangel/conversations2001/4570_pretzels.cfm.
4. Ibid.
5. Ibid.

Four

1. http://library.temple.edu/collections/special_collections/hattie.jsp
2. http://www.verber.com/mark/xian/weight-of-glory.pdf
3. Ibid.

Five

1. http://books.google.com/books?id=EmZi6PiGnTIC&printsec=frontcover&dq
   =Pleasure+and+Profit+in+Bible+Study+and+Anecdotes,+Incidents+and+Illu
   strations+By+D.+L.+Moody&hl=en&ei=3T74TfD9MKrbiAK9tcz9DA&sa=X
   &oi=book_result&ct=result&resnum=1&ved=0CCoQ6AEwAA#v=onepage&
   q&f=false, P.55
2. http://thinkexist.com/quotation/when_you_have_come_to_the_edge_of_all_
   light_that/173385.html
3. Elisabeth Elliot, *Through Gates of Splendor* (New York: Harper & Brothers
   Publishers, 1957); Russell T. Hitt, *Jungle Pilot* (Grand Rapids, MI: Zondervan, 1973); Steve Saint, *End of the Spear* (Carol Stream, IL: SaltRiver Publishers, 2007); "Did They Have to Die?," *Christianity Today Magazine* vol. 40,
   no. 10, 20.

Six

1. http://thinkexist.com/quotation/when_you_get_into_a_tight_place_and_every
   thing/150745.html
2. http://www.explorefaith.org/music/cash.html
3. *Christian History* ("William Carey, 19th Century Missionary to China"), issue 36 (October 1992).

Seven

1. http://www.inspirational-quotes-and-gift-ideas.com/quotes_about_prayer.html
2. Ibid.
3. http://www.prayerfoundation.org/booktexts/z_embounds_powerthroughprayer_
   04.htm

Eight

1. http://www.brainyquote.com/quotes/quotes/s/saintteres209869.html
2. http://www.christiansquoting.org.uk/quotes_by_author_t.htm
3. http://www.debauthor.com/snowtire.htm; used by permission.
4. http://dailychristianquote.com/dcqobedience.html
5. Feldinger, Lauren Gelfond. "Back to Entebbe." *Jerusalem Post Online Edition*
   29 June 2006. See also http://fr.jpost.com/servlet/Satellite?cid=115088587954
   4&pagename=JPost%2FJPArticle%2FPrinter.

𝒩ine

1. http://www.lightoflife.com/LOL_SeekAndYouShallFind.htm
2. http://www.biblesociety.org.uk/about-bible-society/history/mary-jones/
3. Barbara Rainey, *Growing Together in Gratitude* (Little Rock, AR: Family Life, 2010), 19.
4. http://www.lightoflife.com/LOL_SeekAndYouShallFind.htm

𝒯en

1. *Christian History*, vol. 7, no. 4, issue 20.
2. David Jones and Mary Medford. *Richard of Chichester: Bishop 1245–53 . . . Canonized 1262* (Otter Memorial Papers), ed. Paul Foster (West Sussex, England: University of Chichester, 2009) 78–83
3. http://www.bookrags.com/notes/daf/QUO.html, quote no. 18

𝒯leven

1. Andy Andrews, *The Traveler's Gift* (Nashville, TN: Thomas Nelson, 2002), 48–50.
2. Elizabeth Silance Ballard, *Three Letters from Teddy and Other Stories* (Timberlake, NC: Righter Publishing, 2000). [Permission needed?]

𝒯welve

1. As quoted in C. S. Lewis, *A Year with C. S. Lewis: Daily Readings from His Classic Works* (New York: HarperOne, 2003), 149.
2. http://www.holocaustforgotten.com/sendler.htm
3. Hannah Whitall Smith, *The Christian's Secret of a Happy Life*, http://www.worldinvisible.com/library/hwsmith/haplife/cs3.htm.
4. Barbara Rainey, *Growing Together in Courage* (Little Rock, AR: Family Life, 2010), 12.

𝒯hirteen

1. http://www.nouwenlegacy.com/
2. C. S. Lewis, *The Last Battle* (Norwalk, CT: Easton Press with permission of HarperCollins), 210.
3. http://www.suntreeumc.org/pdf%20sermons/Terri_Heroes%20of%20the%20Faith%20Fanny%20Crosby.pdf
4. Story retold from Debbie Macomber, *The Trouble with Angels* (New York: Avon Books, 1994).

Fourteen

1. Harry Berger Jr., "Sprezzatura and the Absence of Grace," in *The Book of the Courtier: The Singleton Translation*, ed. Daniel Javitch (New York: Norton, 2002), 297.
2. Isak Dinesen, *Babette's Feast* (New York: Penguin Books, 2011).
3. Frederick Buechner, *Wishful Thinking: A Seeker's ABC* (San Francisco: Harper San Francisco, 1993), 119.

Fifteen

1. http://quotes.lucywho.com/helen-keller-quotes-t52776.html
2. Rick Warren, *The Purpose Driven Life* (Grand Rapids, MI: Zondervan, 2002), 17.

Sixteen

1. http://www.spiritoffire.org/ebooks/how%20to%20pray/pray07.htm, chapter 7, section 2.
2. Cheri Fuller, *The One Year Book of Praying Through the Bible* (Carol Stream, IL: Tyndale House Publishers, Inc., 2003), introduction.

DISCUSSION QUESTIONS FOR
ONE PERFECT WORD

1. What is it about choosing just one word to chew on for a whole year that seems like such an adventure? Have you ever had a word or an idea crop up again and again over a short period of time? What was that word or idea? Why do you think it kept surfacing?

2. In 1977, the word that kept cropping up for Debbie was the word *desire*. What does that word conjure up for you? If you could name one desire—a secret dream—for your life, what would it be? (Don't be afraid to dream big.)

3. For Debbie, the word *believe* came at a time of great uncertainty, right at the turn of the millennium with all the hype of Y2K. Does this give us insight into God's timing as he gives us a word assignment? Why do you think he gave Debbie the word *believe* when she was facing misgivings and fear? Why not *courage* or another buck-up type word?

4. Debbie confessed that she chose *hunger* in 1979 as she struggled with her eating addiction. She thought the word would take her one place, but she ended up learning something entirely different. Has that ever happened to you?

Have you ever set out thinking you were going to explore one thing only to find out God had a different plan? What was the surprise lesson you learned?

5. The year 1986 was a troubled one for Debbie. Why do you think God chose *trust*? Do you see God's hand in the choice of words? Do you think we are somehow asking for trouble when we choose a word that only grows out of challenges? You've heard people jokingly advise, "Never pray for patience. You'll only get trials." Is there an upside to choosing a potentially difficult word?

6. During one of the toughest years in Debbie's life, her word was *brokenness*. Look back over your life. Was there a year that seemed to reflect that theme, even if you didn't intentionally choose it? How did God work through that with you?

7. In 1990, Debbie chose the word *prayer*. Have you ever had a yearlong adventure in prayer? If you were to choose this word, how would you explore it? How does one move *prayer* from the coulda-woulda-shoulda list to the just-can't-get-enough-of-this list?

8. When you saw that Debbie picked the word *obedience* in 1998, what was your reaction? It's not exactly a motivational word, is it? Debbie says, "We need to recognize that if we ignore His rules, there will be consequences." Why is obedience so difficult for us, especially when we consider that it will save us untold chaos?

9. In 2002, Debbie's word was *seek*. She believes it's been a theme for much of her life. What happens to us when we

seek God? How do we go about doing this? How might our lives be different if we were never called to seek God?

10. When Debbie chose the word *balance* in 2009, did you identify with her? What is it that keeps us off balance in this hectic world? If you could somehow find balance, what would it look like? How do we take steps to get our life in balance?

11. Wisdom is one of those things God promises to give us if we ask. In this age of quick judgment, impetuous actions, and on-the-spot decision making, how do we cultivate wisdom? Think of the people you know? Describe your wisest friend. What sets that person apart?

12. In 2004, Debbie was surprised by the word that came to her: *surrender.* Have you ever been surprised by something God seemed to have in store for you? How hard is it to surrender to His agenda? When we work so diligently to keep control, is it scary to consider surrender? What does it take to get there?

13. It was 2006 that Debbie's word was *hope.* She found out it was very different from simple optimism. What is the difference? How do we learn to hope?

14. *Passion* is an exciting word. When Debbie chose it, she already knew she was a person who embraced things in a big way. During the year she learned that the world is sometimes uncomfortable with passion. It's not cool. How do we give up the cool detachment that is thought to be attractive? How do we stop holding back? Do we worry that if we be-

come passionate people we will somehow burn out? What does God have to say about this?

15. Debbie explored the word *purpose* a couple of years ago. The yearlong study took her some interesting places. Do you believe God has one big purpose for your life like he did for Esther? Or are our lives made up of many opportunities— many purposes? How do we find our place? What holds us back from realizing our potential?

16. Were you surprised to see all the verses used throughout the book that had promises attached? Why is it we hold back from seeking all God has promised us? Is it that we think we are not worthy? Are we afraid to take the Lord literally? Look through the verses Debbie outlined in chapter sixteen. Rewrite them into your journal—one a day— putting your own name in each one, personalizing them like this: *If SUSIE remains in me and my words remain in HER, SHE CAN ask whatever SHE wishes, and it will be done for HER (John 15:7)*. Meditate on these powerful promises.

A Conversation With Debbie Macomber

Do you think of meditating on a single word as a private journey, or is it more of a shared experience for you?

It's more of a private journey.

Do you still meet every week with your breakfast club? What is your favorite thing to eat for breakfast?

Now that all of my friends are retired, we meet for lunch instead of breakfast because they are no longer willing to get up as early as me. No matter where we chose to dine in the breakfast days, our favorite choice was oatmeal.

You've framed your own selection of words in the context of your personal faith journey. For readers who are not religious, how do you recommend they discover their perfect words?

I believe God speaks to us no matter where we are in our spiritual journey. I would suggest they keep the ears of their heart open and wait. Their word will come to them, and after seeing it several times, they will recognize it.

***One Perfect Word* examines your spiritual development and growth from a deeply personal perspective. In many cases you share excerpts from your journals. In the**

course of writing this book, how did you feel about sharing such intimate details with your readers?

I don't have a problem with sharing my humanness. I am flawed. I want my readers to understand that I am genuine and sincere and far from perfect. When I share my struggles, my weaknesses with my readers, it helps them know my heart. If they know my heart, then they will recognize my faith and hopefully that will show them the path to God and His love.

At any point in a given year, have you felt unsure about how to proceed with the word you have chosen? What do you recommend for readers who encounter this difficulty?

At times I have felt like I've been left to wander in the desert with my word. I feel that I've done about as much with it as I can. I've studied the definition, I've searched for it through Scripture. It's at that point that I turn it over to God and ask Him, what now?

How has choosing one word for your focus each year simplified your life, and how has it complicated it?

I don't see it as a simplification or a complication. It's a help that keeps me focused and thoughtful. Choosing a word for the year is a help in my spiritual life, a guide that helps me to keep centered.

What are some of the most rewarding aspects of devoting your attention to one word for an entire year?

For me the most rewarding aspect is the communication having a word for the year opens up between God and me. The very first day of the year I turn to Him for direction and guidance while I seek my new word (if He hasn't already given it to me). It opens my heart and my mind to what He has in store for me and what it is He wants me to learn.

Have you ever repeated a word over your many years of this practice? If not, would you ever consider it?
To this point I haven't repeated a word, but that doesn't mean that I won't be open to doing so.

You write that your normal routine is to rise at 3:55 A.M. to begin your day with prayer and Bible study. Can you describe the role self-discipline plays in your relationship with God? What role does it play in your professional success as an author?
Actually I believe I could write an entire book on the benefits of starting my day by spending this time with the Lord. The rewards are staggering. This book is one of the results. If I hadn't had my devotional time there wouldn't be a word for the year. No one can dig into God's Word without reaping abundance. As for self-discipline . . . really what it boils down to is habit, and once cultivated it becomes part of my daily routine.

You write about the importance of setting goals in life. What encouragement can you offer to those who struggle to set and attain goals?
What I normally advise those who are starting to work with goals is to start with baby steps. Don't look beyond what you can achieve or burden yourself with such lofty goals that you set yourself up for failure. Step by step. A little at a time until one is comfortable setting priorities.

Do you know what your word for next year will be?
I do. The word is *magnify*.

Also by

DEBBIE MACOMBER

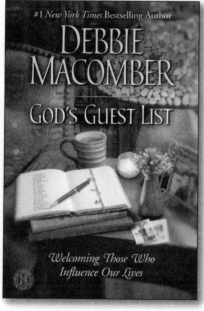 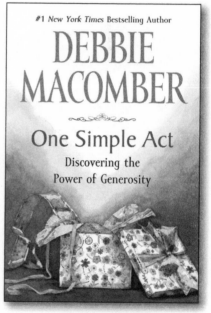

God's Guest List
Hardcover: 9781439108963
Trade Paper: 9781439190647

One Simple Act
Hardcover: 9781439108932
Trade Paper: 9781439109373

AVAILABLE WHEREVER BOOKS ARE SOLD OR AT
WWW.SIMONANDSCHUSTER.COM

HOWARD BOOKS
A Division of Simon & Schuster
A CBS COMPANY